Conten

List of abbreviations

ACPC	area child protection committee
ADCS	Association of Directors of Children's Services
CAADA	Co-ordinated Action Against Domestic Abuse
CAF	common assessment framework
CAFCASS	Child and Family Court Advisory Support Service
CAMHS	Child and Adolescent Mental Health Services
CPIA	Criminal Procedure and Investigations Act 1996
CPS	Crown Prosecution Service
CQC	Care Quality Commission
CSCI	Commission for Social Care Inspection (replaced by CQC)
CSSIW	Care and Social Services Inspectorate Wales
DCFS	Department for Children and Family Services (US government department)
DCS	director of children's services
DfE	Department for Education
DfES	Department for Education and Skills (2001–07)
DH	Department of Health
DHR	domestic homicide review
DVRIM	domestic violence risk identification matrix
EPPE	effective provision of pre-school education
ESTYN	Welsh Inspectorate for Education and Training
FE	further education
FIP	family intervention project
GP	General Practitioner
HPC	Health Professions Council
IMR	individual management review
IPV	intimate partner violence
IYSS	integrated youth support services
LILAC	Leading Improvements for Looked After Children
LSCB	local safeguarding children board
MARAC	multi-agency risk assessment conference
MASH	multi-agency safeguarding hub

MST	Multi-systemic Therapy
NCI/ NCISH	National Confidential Inquiry into Suicide and Homicide by People with Mental Illness
NHS	National Health Service
NPSA	National Patient Safety Agency
NSPCC	National Society for the Prevention of Cruelty to Children
OBA	outcomes-based accountability
PCT	primary care trust
RCA	root cause analysis
SCIE	Social Care Institute for Excellence
SCR	serious case review
SHA	strategic health authority
UKBA	United Kingdom Border Agency
UNCRC	United Nations Convention on the Rights of the Child
YOT	youth offending team

Notes on contributors

Maggie Blyth is independent chair of Kent Safeguarding Children Board and Herefordshire Safeguarding Children Board. She has held public office as a member of the Parole Board for England and Wales since 2005 and the UK Health Professions Council since 2010. Between 2007 and 2009 she was independent chair of Nottingham Youth Offending Team Board. Maggie was a senior civil servant at the Youth Justice Board until 2005, which included oversight of child deaths in custody. Her professional background is as a senior manager in youth justice services and previously as a teacher, and her specialist knowledge is related to work with high-risk young people. She has jointly edited four books for The Policy Press.

Enver Solomon is director of policy and public affairs at the Children's Society. He has extensive experience of lobbying government and influencing policy to improve outcomes, particularly for the most disadvantaged children. He has worked in a number of voluntary organisations, including Barnardo's, the Revolving Doors Agency and the Centre for Crime and Justice Studies, and has a particular interest in the youth justice system, looked-after children and child protection. Enver has published a number of policy reports and jointly edited three books for The Policy Press. Before working in policy, he was a BBC journalist for 10 years.

Jenny Clifton is principal policy advisor on safeguarding for the Children's Commissioner for England. She is a qualified social worker and has worked in practice, management and lead policy roles in local government and the voluntary sector, with a focus chiefly on children. She has held posts as university lecturer in social work and social policy and has published on children's rights and on domestic violence. Jenny's current work concerns the promotion of children's and young people's rights to protection, their perspectives on the child protection process, and how they might be enabled to access help at an earlier stage.

Andrew Coombe is associate director of safeguarding at NHS Kent and Medway. His professional background is as a registered general and psychiatric nurse and he has extensive experience working in the field of mental health both as a manager and a commissioner. More recently, he worked with GPs in developing practice-based commissioning, a precursor of the current NHS reforms, before moving into the area of safeguarding children and vulnerable adults. Last year he was awarded an MA Health Services Research by the University of Kent.

John Fox is a former detective superintendent and head of child abuse investigation in the Hampshire Constabulary. He has represented the Association of Chief Police Officers on various government working parties and committees concerning child abuse and related issues, and he was Lord Laming's police advisor and assessor on the Victoria Climbié Inquiry. In recent years, he has chaired various SCR panels and acted as overview author. He has an MSc Criminology and Criminal Justice from the University of Surrey and is currently working towards a PhD.

Colin Green took up post as director of children's services for Coventry City Council in January 2007. Immediately prior to this, he worked for the DfES for three years with policy lead for safeguarding children and before that was assistant director for children's services in Cambridgeshire. Colin is a social worker by professional background, and over his career has worked with all age groups and in a wide variety of practitioner and management roles. He is also chair of the national ADCS Families, Communities and Young People's Policy Committee.

Amanda Holt is a senior lecturer in criminological psychology at the Institute of Criminal Justice Studies at the University of Portsmouth. She teaches across a range of undergraduate and postgraduate programmes in criminology, psychology and forensic studies and her research background involves work with young people and families in the fields of health, education and youth justice. Recent research projects address adolescent-to-parent abuse, anti-violence strategies in schools and pluralities in qualitative data analysis. Amanda is currently writing a book about family violence for The Policy Press.

Michael Preston-Shoot is professor of social work and dean of the Faculty of Health and Social Sciences, University of Bedfordshire. He is independent chair of Luton Safeguarding Children Board and of Luton Safeguarding Adults Board. He is one of the founding editors of the journal *Ethics and Social Welfare* and has researched and published widely on the interface between law, education and training, and professional practice. Michael has recently completed research for the Department of Health, published by the Social Care Institute for Excellence, on the governance of safeguarding adults boards.

Gwyther Rees is research director for the Children's Society and a visiting associate at the Social Policy Research Unit, University of York. He has contributed to two recent studies on child protection issues relating to young people aged 11 to 17, both undertaken for a partnership comprising the Children's Society, the University of York and NSPCC, and is lead author of a book on adolescent neglect. Gwyther's other main areas of research are young runaways and children's subjective wellbeing.

Mike Stein is a research professor in the Social Policy Research Unit at the University of York. He directed the Neglected Adolescents research project, funded by the DfE and DH Safeguarding Children Research Initiative. He specialises in the problems and challenges faced by young people living in and leaving care, vulnerable adolescents, and young people running away from care. Mike has published extensively in the field (see www.york.ac.uk/spru), and his latest book, *Care Less Lives*, tells the story of the rights movement of young people in care (www.leavingcare.org).

Acknowledgements

We would like to thank everyone who contributed to this publication and in particular Janice for her faultless editing. The views expressed in this volume are varied and do not necessarily reflect the views of the editors. We are grateful to all the contributors for adding to an important debate concerning children and young people in the child protection system. We would like to thank Dr Maggie Atkinson, the Children's Commissioner for England, for her foreword to our volume.

Foreword

I am pleased to provide the foreword to this timely collection of different professionals' views on the chances of successful implementation of the reforms proposed by Professor Eileen Munro.

I was heartened by the Professor's insistence that the child's concerns, timeframes, voice and views should be at the heart of work done to safeguard and protect them. Central to all our concerns must be the wellbeing and life chances of the children on whose circumstances our work focuses. We do them, and in the end ourselves, a disservice if we put our professional concerns and administrative, regulatory or bureaucratic demands before the paramount requirement that we meet children's needs, wishes and aspirations.

A striking theme in every chapter that follows is how easy we have found it, over years of developing ever more accountable ways of working, to place the child at the centre of our concerns, shaping our planning, service design and delivery, spending and regulation around that focal point. Even advantaged and well-supported children cannot level the playing field of opportunity for themselves. For the vast majority, those who smooth the way, ensuring they have rich opportunities to succeed, are their families, their schools and the people in their communities. The vulnerable children and families with whom targeted safeguarding and specialist child protection services work are much further away from enjoying those chances. We must step in and create these opportunities for and preferably with them.

We owe it to children to take Professor Munro's conclusions seriously. This means not simply reading, agreeing with and noting voices, views and reported lived experiences. It means taking up the challenges, affirming what we do that already delivers and, where necessary, changing what we do and how and with whom we work to make good what we are challenged to ensure.

We must remind ourselves that children, all of them vulnerable because they are children and some far more challenging because of what the adult world visits on their young lives, without exception, have the support they need and the right to be heard. Nothing less will do. They are the rights we promise to uphold and the promises we make to our children.

Dr Maggie Atkinson
Children's Commissioner for England
October 2011

Introduction

Maggie Blyth and Enver Solomon

There have been many pivotal moments in the recent history of child protection. In the past few years, they have followed the tragic death of a young child and led to wide-ranging reviews, most recently the Laming Inquiry in 2009 following the death of Baby Peter in Haringey. However, the independent review of child protection by Professor Eileen Munro, which concluded in May 2011, was initiated as a response to a change in government policy. Government ministers responded swiftly to Munro's recommendations in July 2011, broadly accepting that all her proposals would be dealt with 'in the round' (DfE, 2011). To many working in the sector, this feels like a critical point when child protection could take a different direction. There are, clearly, many questions to be raised and lots of points for discussion. This volume intends to provide space for these to be aired and to help all interested parties think though the implications of the Munro Review and the government's response.

There are three core themes to the contributions. First, solid evidence has to be the driver for good policy. This applies to understanding what works in child protection and can be implemented by local authorities and their partners. Second, any review of the child protection system in this country must focus on the child rather than the system. And third, the effective protection of children and young people involves sound judgements of risk at both a practice and organisational level. Working predominantly with very vulnerable children, this last proviso can present challenges to everyone within children's services, particularly at a time when the reorganisation of public services is impacting on the configuration of resources at the 'front door'. Moreover, changes to the health economy, reforms to education and the reorganisation facing some police public protection teams will inevitably compound what Professor Munro has described as a 'commonly held belief that the complexity and associated uncertainty of child protection work can be eradicated' (Munro, 2011b).

In May 2011, Professor Eileen Munro published her final report in her review of the child protection system. *A child-centred system* (Munro, 2011b) makes a number of recommendations for government and the multi-agency child protection system. In July 2011, the government responded to the 15 recommendations Munro identified for reform by adopting all the principles she proposed for an effective child protection system (DfE, 2011).

There are four clear assumptions that underpin Munro's review and the government response. First, there is recognition of the importance of valuing professional expertise, and as a consequence a radical reduction in regulation has begun, including revisions to *Working together* (DfE, 2010), a new inspection framework (Ofsted, 2011b) and a reduction in central prescription in favour of professional judgement, particularly in relation to assessing need. Second, children should be protected from abuse and neglect in the first place and local arrangements must be in place to identify those children most at risk, with the offer of 'early help'. Third, all social work students should be well prepared for the challenges of child protection work and the regulation of qualified social workers will move to the Health Professions Council (HPC), with improved social work training. A new principal child and family social worker will be created at a local level, with a chief social worker provided at Whitehall. Finally, the 'challenge' role of local safeguarding children boards (LSCBs) will be strengthened to ensure the ongoing statutory, multi-agency oversight of safeguarding. The government has stated that LSCBs have a 'unique, system-wide, role to play in protecting children and young people' (Munro, 2011b). LSCBs will also be expected to use systems methodology when undertaking serious case reviews (SCRs).

The government has established a Children's Improvement Board to implement much of the longer-term reform of the child protection system and funding has been made available through this body to assist in the phased introduction of the reforms to support local transition areas. The Munro Review final report makes clear that inspection and the role of Ofsted will continue to form part of any overall improvement system but there will be potential for less inspection as the sector-led approach develops.

Munro's review and the government response have been broadly welcomed by policymakers, practitioners and academics working within safeguarding. The value placed on professional expertise, the shared responsibility for the provision of early help to children and young people, the development of social work practice, and strengthening accountability at local level make sense. But in what ways do the Munro Review and the government's response offer concrete solutions to key dilemmas facing agencies working in the child protection system? What does Munro provide in terms of improving outcomes for children at a time when the numbers entering the child protection system have escalated? How does the Munro Review help agencies involved in child protection understand thresholds, referral decisions and a common understanding of levels of need? And will the recommendations that government has broadly accepted, albeit to be implemented 'in the round', promote the learning so desperately needed to prevent children and young people being harmed and abused in our society?

The reflections of our expert contributors, who come from practice, policy and academia, are intended to provide important critical appraisal of government policy in relation to the Munro Review. The chapters consider the emphasis on self-improvement for children's services, with the opportunities for taking sector-led responsibility for performance, against the reality that in a climate of significantly reduced public sector resources, coupled with a significant increase in child protection cases, there are huge pressures on local services and frontline practitioners. They raise some important questions about effective multi-agency working, that is, all statutory agencies tasked with child protection duties, including voluntary and community organisations which may be in place to provide early support. Is the offer of early support the right approach to addressing problems at an earlier stage of the child's journey and will adopting such a strategy prevent the numbers of children entering the child protection system from continuing to rise? And what are the lessons for how services should be configured and delivered to ensure that all children are safe and protected, including those groups of vulnerable older adolescents, young carers and children who suffer hidden harm as a result of parental mental health problems or substance misuse.

The earlier the better?

Early intervention was a defining feature of Labour's approach to working with children and young people at risk (Blyth and Solomon, 2009). Munro has coined the term 'early help' and Colin Green examines what this means in his evaluation of the success of prevention services over the past decade in improving outcomes for the most vulnerable children (Chapter 1). While there may be broad agreement that access to mainstream services should be prioritised for children, young people and their families in deprived areas, early intervention projects have been affected by recent public sector deficits. Green concludes that the prospects for delivering the early offer of help do not look promising in the current economic climate and in the absence of a clear body of research that supports policymakers and practitioners in distinguishing what works from what makes no difference in improving outcomes for vulnerable children. Green emphasises the need to use evidence-based practice in determining policy and highlights the need for greater understanding of why numbers of children subject to child protection plans have increased after a decade of investment in prevention services.

In his contribution about the effectiveness of LSCBs, Michael Preston-Shoot (Chapter 2) provides a literature review of all the studies available on the effectiveness of LSCBs and concludes that there is limited evidence of improved outcomes for children and young people (France et al, 2010; Ofsted, 2011a). However, he concedes that being able to hold local partnerships to account through an independent chair can deliver public confidence and it is clear from the studies available that the achievements of LSCBs are 'commendable'.

Voice of the child

Munro's second report published in February 2011 (Munro, 2011a) considered the child's journey through the child protection system – from early contact and referrals from other agencies or people through to assessment, intervention and receiving help. It concluded that the child protection system too often overlooks the voice of the child and that the lack of available social work expertise can result in inappropriate referrals from other professionals. Jenny Clifton, in her review of a study undertaken by the Office of the Children's Commissioner (Chapter 3), reports that 'children and young people wanted to make sense of the system in which they were involved'. She outlines three prerequisites for ensuring that children are seen and heard within the child protection system. As with wider children's services, the challenge will be to ensure that those young people most at risk are prioritised in gaining access to universal provision, most notably education and health services.

In October 2011, David Cameron appointed Louise Casey to lead the new Troubled Families Team within the Department of Communities and Local Government to drive cross-government policy and delivery aiming to ensure that the identification and targeting of the 'dysfunctional' or 'problem family' is at the heart of all domestic policy. Although it is not clear how such a policy will be integrated into the challenges outlined by the Munro Review, or whether problem behaviour can be separated out from the circumstances in which families live, there is clearly a strong commitment to maintaining a focus on prevention services. The Prime Minister has also offered his support to the development of an Early Intervention Foundation promoted by the work of Graham Allen (Allen, 2011).

Multi-agency working

'A major challenge in building a more responsive child protection system is helping a wide range of professions to work together well in order to build an accurate understanding of what is happening in the child or young person's life, so the right help can be provided', writes Munro in her final report. Her review acknowledges the association between child abuse and neglect and the impact of mental illness, domestic violence and substance misuse, but it is arguable whether Munro provides real guidance on how to integrate more effectively adult and children's services. Andrew Coombe (Chapter 4) describes the difficulties children and families face because the needs of children are overlooked when assessing adult capability. Coombe, with a focus on the impact of parental mental illness on children, draws on findings from a number of national and local studies on SCRs, which demonstrate repeatedly the poor information exchange between adult and children's services in relation to mental health issues.

Similar themes are drawn out by Amanda Holt (Chapter 5), who describes how the 'hidden yet prevalent problem' of parental abuse is perpetuated by misunderstandings within children's services that adolescent-on-parent violence is associated more with behavioural problems or poor parenting than other traditional forms of domestic abuse. She demonstrates the difficulty for different agencies in understanding such abuse in the context of family violence and offers a challenge to social policy to use the Munro Review to 'decide what kind of problem (and whose problem) adolescent-to-parent abuse is'. Stein and Rees (Chapter 6) explore how the needs of 11 to 17 year olds are not always met by child protection processes, which are more geared to protecting younger children. Making similar observations to Coombe and Holt, they remain concerned that without a clear understanding of 'children in need' policies at local level, some older adolescents will fail to attract supportive interventions and instead drift into the youth justice system, go missing, become homeless or become transparent to the system.

Strengthening accountability of safeguarding across the partnership

In light of the difficulties and complexities of multi-agency responses to children, young people and their families who may need support, Munro has argued that it is vital that there continue to be clear lines of accountability for child protection as the Coalition government's plans for reform in the public services are implemented. In moving to a system that promotes the exercise of professional judgement, local multi-agency systems will need to get better at monitoring, learning and adapting their practice.

The government has acknowledged that LSCBs remain uniquely positioned and accountable across local agencies and communities to provide oversight of how the child protection system is working and that they should draw on nationally and locally collected performance information to benchmark performance. Their statutory remit will continue post-Munro and they will increasingly be expected to perform a scrutiny role, to identify emerging practice challenges and areas for improvement and development. However, LSCBs are only effective if the services over which they have oversight are able to function effectively. Michael Preston-Shoot (Chapter 2) is concerned that insufficient consideration has been given to the reorganisation of the public sector currently under way and the impact of that on child protection practice. He believes that the commitment to improving social work practice may be undermined by lack of resource at local level and considers the Munro reforms to be 'essentially cosmetic, missing an opportunity for critique and a rethinking of mandate, partnership structures and resources'. Similarly, John Fox (Chapter 7) is concerned that, in promoting systems methodology when undertaking SCRs, there may be limitations to the way in which lessons learned are disseminated to improve practice. He argues that SCRs have the mandate to identify what happened and why when a child dies or suffers harm and to provide 'rigorous and independent' evaluations.

A new dawn for child protection?

For many working in the field of child protection, the Munro Review is a welcome development and has certainly been hailed by some contributors (Holt, Chapter 5; Coombe, Chapter 4) as providing opportunities to clarify particular safeguarding issues. Holt refers to it as a 'watershed'. However, when drilling down into the detail, does it go far enough in its demands of national policy and local practice? We hope the contributions in this book will help all those interested in child protection to think through the implications and critically appraise what the future holds.

References

Allen, G. (2011) *Early intervention: The next steps*, London: Department for Work and Pensions (DWP).

Blyth, M. and Solomon, E. (2009) *Young people and prevention*, Bristol: The Policy Press.

DfE (Department for Education) (2010) *Working together to safeguard children: A guide to inter-agency working to safeguard and promote the welfare of children*, London: The Stationery Office.

DfE (2011) *A child-centred system: The government's response to the Munro Review of Child Protection*, London: The Stationery Office. Available at: www.education.gov.uk/publications.

France, A., Munro, E.R. and Waring, A. (2010) *The evaluation of arrangements for effective operation of the new local safeguarding children boards in England: Final report*, London: Department for Children, Schools and Families (DCSF).

Munro, E. (2011a) *The Munro Review of Child Protection: Interim report: The child's journey*, London: The Stationery Office. Available at: www.education.gov.uk/publications.

Munro, E. (2011b) *The Munro Review of Child Protection: Final report, A child-centred system*, London: The Stationery Office. Available at: www.education.gov.uk/publications.

Ofsted (2011a) *Good practice by local safeguarding children boards*, Manchester: Office for Standards in Education, Children's Services and Skills.

Ofsted (2011b) *Common Inspection Framework: Consultation*, Manchester: Office for Standards in Education, Children's Services and Skills.

ONE

Early intervention

Colin Green

Introduction

What do we mean by early intervention? As Eileen Munro (2011) sets out in her review of child protection, the term 'early intervention', or as she prefers 'early help', is ambiguous and open to a wide range of interpretations. In this chapter I will follow her lead and take the term to refer to both intervention early in a child's life and to intervention early in the development of a problem or vulnerability, whatever the age of the child or young person. My focus will be on early intervention in relation to safeguarding children from harm arising from poor or dangerous or neglectful parental care rather than other sources of harm. With that focus, the chapter is aligned to, considers and develops some of the issues raised in chapter 5 of the Munro Review (2011: 69), 'Sharing responsibility for the provision of early help'.

There is a wealth of material on the benefits of early intervention in the scope of the meaning of the term described above. Recent reviews by Graham Allen MP, Dame Clare Tickell and Frank Field, evaluation of the Sure Start programme, the EPPE study and other UK work, as well as considerable historical research from the US and other countries, all support the moral and financial case for various kinds of early intervention (Institute of Education, 1999–2008; DfE, 2002–11; Allen, 2011; Tickell, 2011; Field, 2011). The Marmot Review (Marmot, 2010) demonstrated unequivocally the link between positive early development and whole of life health. The Every Child Matters programme was based on the premise that the best protection for all children is through access to high-quality universal services, the most comprehensive form of early help. Past and current government focus on educational attainment is the most visible expression of this. It is based on the strong evidence that education can be life-changing, that attainment at 16 years is a key indicator of life chances and that there are links between wider health and wellbeing and educational attainment. We have evidence of the positive impact of targeted programmes such as the Family Nurse Partnership, the Reading Recovery programme and the positive parenting (Triple P) programme developed by the Parent and Family Support Centre at the University of Queensland. There is also a range of more specialist programmes such as Multisystemic Therapy (MST), family intervention projects (FIPs) and developments such as the Swindon Family LIFE programme, all of which have a growing evidence base for effectiveness.

Benefits of intervening early

All of these programmes appear to show impressive returns on investment. In his second report, Graham Allen (2011) develops the economic case for early intervention in some detail and outlines potential models for attracting investment in early intervention.

Given this developing evidence base and the very substantial investment in early intervention and in universal services over the past decade or so, it begs the question as to why those agencies and organisations which work with children and families have not more wholeheartedly adopted the methods shown to have the most impact. In addition, we must consider why all this investment and effort has not produced better results for all children and especially for those who are most vulnerable. International comparisons of children and young people's welfare continue to place English children and young people among the most disadvantaged in the OECD nations, with some of the greatest inequalities (OECD, 2011). In the area of educational attainment, the improvement in results in national tests at key stages 2 and 4 is contested. Even if we accept that overall levels of attainment have significantly improved, the evidence suggests that any narrowing of the gap between vulnerable children and young people and others has been minimal and for some groups the gap may have become wider.

If we consider the more specific area of child protection, there is no evidence that the need for child protection services has diminished. If anything, the evidence points in the other direction. In spite of the huge investment in Sure Start, schools, young people's services through Connexions and integrated youth support services (IYSS), the number of children with child protection plans has increased from 25,900 in 2004/05 to 42,300 in 2010/11. This is an increase of 63%. The numbers of referrals to children's social care have increased over the same period, from 552,000 to 613,000, and numbers of initial assessments from 293,000 to 441,000, an increase of 34% (DfE and BIS, 2011). At the sharpest end of child protection work, the evidence points to more need, as the figures for children subject to care proceedings have risen by more than 40% since 2008/09 and continue to rise (CAFCASS, 2011). I do not think we can just see this as an effect of the Peter Connelly case. The rise started before the case attracted widespread public attention, and unlike the rises in activity following other high-profile cases such as Victoria Climbié this rise has been sustained; the latest figures from CAFCASS indicate that over two years later the level of activity is still rising.

What do we make of this conflicting evidence for the benefits of early intervention of various kinds against a lack of impact on outcomes at population level and for the most vulnerable children and young people who require a child protection service? This is in a context of sharply reduced public expenditure, especially for local authorities and the police, severe pressure on NHS budgets and likely increased pressure on school budgets. For hard-pressed local authority directors of finance, promises of savings in the mid-term or savings that accrue to other agencies do not cut much ice. They are looking for changes in services that will have an impact on expenditure now.

Have early intervention services in children's services made a difference? The macro evidence on the impact of early intervention thus far is weak. However, this is an area where evaluation and judgements of impact are inherently difficult, not least as the interventions are taking place in a very dynamic social and economic environment. Our population has changed markedly over the past 10 years. We are in the middle of the worst recession for 70 years. There is no doubt that there is less social solidarity than before, with more fragmented families and greater expectation that the state will solve problems which might previously have been seen as solely the preserve of family members or the community to resolve. Our ideas on what is acceptable care for children have changed as our knowledge of what is harmful has developed. Graham Allen (2011) makes particular use of the evidence of the impact of the quality of care of babies and young children on brain development. There is a much better focus on the impact of domestic violence on children and young people and we have improved our understanding of the risks to missing children and of sexual exploitation of children and young people.

One hypothesis is that the increased resources for early intervention have led to more identification of need and to the identification of children in need of protection. Nearly all local authorities have changed their services to provide a wider range of response: for example, the development of processes and resources to support implementation of the common assessment framework, development of referral and assessment services to provide a better front door, and work to ensure that thresholds for intervention are well understood across the whole network of local agencies and services.

Evidence from inspection would suggest that most local authorities are offering better child protection responses. The current inspection framework is the tightest to date in its focus on this area of service, and while its sharpest focus is on local authority services, it also gives a clear picture of NHS and police service contributions to child protection and safeguarding services. I believe the inspection process has raised standards, though it is of concern that local authorities are still receiving 'inadequate' judgements for their safeguarding services more than two years into the inspection programme. Ofsted (2011) published an analysis of inspection outcomes which suggested that far fewer local authorities were judged inadequate during the last year of inspection than in the first. However, there was bias in the selection of authorities for inspection in the first year towards those where there was concern about the quality of services.

My conclusion is that we may have the paradox of better early intervention and better identification of need, which leads to more child protection responses as more need is identified, and that those responses are also better.

Early intervention and child protection

The Munro Review offered a very positive view of the potential of early intervention to improve outcomes for children and young people who need help. The review drew on the sources referred to above to make the moral and financial case for early intervention. In chapter five, 'Sharing responsibility for the provision of early help', it made the case for the importance of engaging universal and targeted services in the identification of children and young people who need help, including those who may be at risk of or are being harmed. The review's analysis that earlier intervention leads to better outcomes is sound.

What is much more difficult to establish is whether the kinds of early intervention which the Munro Review describes and others promote have the ability to make a difference to that relatively small number of children and young people living in families with serious difficulties that lead to child protection plans and care proceedings. What Munro does advocate is that, whatever the difficulty, it is best identified and addressed early and in that sense she must be right. In child development terms, we must provide help to those families and their children where there are the most serious risks of poor outcomes as soon as possible.

Munro correctly identifies that there remain significant problems in coordinating services and in the confidence of universal and targeted services in identifying and working with children who are or may be abused and neglected. The review identifies a number of approaches to strengthening and changing services that could help address these problems. Notably she advocates greater use of lead family workers and the development of multidisciplinary teams acting as first points of contact for those with child and family concerns. These teams would provide expertise to universal and targeted services. In particular, she advocates using social work expertise in evaluating information on potential harm to children and in assisting other services to understand and manage risk and to identify those children and young people who are at risk of harm and require a specialist child protection response. These approaches are being tried in a number of local authorities, which are very positive about their impact on quality of work and improving identification of children at risk of harm.

Munro does not explore how well these approaches work in relation to the genesis of different types of abuse. It is evident that where the issues are of neglect or emotional abuse, that is, matters that tend to develop or be observable over time, these approaches will work. It is less clear how effective they may be at identifying those families where the risk of harm is physical or sexual abuse.

For all forms of early intervention there is the issue of the willingness of those identified as having a need to recognise that need and engage with services. There is substantial evidence that early identification gives more opportunity to engage before problems are entrenched or those who are identified as needing help become entrenched in their view of their problems. For example, the point of engagement with the Family Nurse Partnership is at about 14 weeks into the pregnancy because there is evidence that this is the point where the likelihood of positive engagement is greatest for both mothers and fathers of the baby (DH, 2011a).

Experience from a range of services where those receiving the intervention may be at best ambivalent and at worst hostile has shown that assertive and highly skilled staff can engage in the most unpromising of circumstances, for example, assertive outreach in adult mental health and the MST programme.

Munro recommends a duty on local authorities and statutory partners 'to secure the sufficient provision of local early help services for children, young people and families' to try to ensure that these promising developments are widely implemented (Munro, 2011:78). The recommendation goes on to detail how they should do this. Given that much of the rest of the review advocates the removal of detailed specification of how services should be provided and a reduction in the quantity and specificity of guidance, it seems counterintuitive for the report to recommend a new statutory duty, especially when the government has removed requirements designed to promote effective working together of agencies, such as the requirement for children's trusts and for the production of a Children and Young People's Plan. In its response, the government agreed with the principles of this recommendation but said it would give further consideration to how best to achieve the aim during the summer of 2011 (DfE, 2011). In other words, it did not make any commitment to implement a new statutory duty.

If there were a new duty, or simply if the principles behind this recommendation were widely accepted, what would this mean in practice?

As noted earlier in this chapter, the current financial pressures could make the job of implementing a new duty seem very unpromising. Local authorities and their partners, especially the NHS and police partners, are all required to deliver very substantial savings. The financial pressures also make it more critical than ever that whatever we do to intervene to improve the lives of children, young people and families is effective and delivers the necessary outcomes. All the agencies involved want to make savings in reducing high-cost interventions which are delivered late in the development of a child or young person's difficulty and often deliver the least gain because, by then, problems are entrenched and the child or young person's development has already been significantly impaired.

The Munro Review commends a number of initiatives, such as MASH (multi-agency safeguarding hub) teams and locating social workers in early intervention services to help them manage safeguarding concerns by providing advice and expertise on safeguarding issues and developing the confidence of services in managing risk without referring the child and family on to children's social care (Munro, 2011: 81). All of these developments are at a relatively early stage of implementation, and while evaluation suggests promising results, there is not yet a body of secure evidence of the difference these and other workforce remodelling initiatives can make.

Making early help a reality

If we are to make a reality of early help now when we have not succeeded in delivering sufficient early help over the past 10 years in financially more favourable circumstances, I think we need to address four key issues.

First, we need to reconfigure services in the way the Munro Review suggests. This would mean increasing the capacity of services to identify vulnerable children and young people and to offer them and their families help. In a context of diminishing resources overall, this capacity can only come either from taking resources away from remedial child protection and other services that provide services to the most vulnerable or through universal services taking a greater role in identification of need and then meeting that need through targeted help. In the medium to long term, better early help may release resources from remedial services. To date, the investment in early intervention has not achieved this, so we cannot count on this delivering resources in the immediate or near future.

The resources would need to come from a refocusing of services such as Sure Start children's centres, health visiting, school nursing, school support and youth services towards services targeted at those requiring early help. The direction of government policy for Sure Start (DfE, 2010) and health visiting (DH, 2011b) at least in part supports this, with a greater focus on the most vulnerable and identification of need as early as possible in a child's life through improved screening implemented through the Healthy Child Programme (DH, 2009). The expansion of the Family Nurse Partnership as a targeted programme also supports this approach. What is less clear is whether schools are ready to develop their role further in this direction. With increasing numbers of schools becoming academies and loosening their ties with local authorities, ending their duty to cooperate, and the focus on absolute measures of attainment, there are powerful messages and incentives to schools to focus their efforts away from the most vulnerable children. While there is a great deal of talk about moral purpose in education and the importance of increasing social mobility and closing attainment gaps between the socially advantaged and the socially disadvantaged, there is little sign that even under previous policies this occurred, with their focus on the disadvantaged and disadvantaged communities, for example the original academies programme that focused on low-attaining schools almost all in very disadvantaged communities. I expect this to be even harder with market-based reforms, which by their nature will favour those with the greatest resources, whether these are material wealth, information or motivation.

Second, if the way to deliver early help is through refocusing existing universal and targeted services, how might this be done? It is evident that this requires partnership working. The Every Child Matters reforms sought to build partnership and integrated working into the framework for delivery of children's services. It was always envisaged that it would be a 10-year programme to achieve the cultural changes and outcomes sought. The programme, as government policy, has been halted about two thirds of the way through this time period. Some of the levers that helped partners work together have been removed. There is an argument that effective partnership is built on common purpose, shared objectives, effective joint performance management and shared incentives for change, not on whether there is a legislative duty in place or not. There is a good deal of truth in this. However, the signals from government are important, especially those delivered through the performance management and inspection frameworks for the key services in this area. All these are in varying states of flux. The inspection framework for local authorities' work in safeguarding children remains robust. However, it has a limited focus on 'early help'. The framework for schools has been amended to focus on a narrower range of issues (Ofsted, 2011). While safeguarding children and young people remains central, the general message is that the focus is on attainment, progress, quality of teaching and leadership, rather than the wider role of the school in its community and its welfare responsibilities for children and young people.

There is wide concern that the changes in the NHS will weaken the focus on safeguarding. It is not yet clear how some of the key safeguarding roles in the current arrangements, such as designated and named nurses and doctors, will be commissioned in the new structures. Without an infrastructure to support safeguarding and child protection work, including supporting the provision of early help as a safeguarding role, it is hard to see how NHS bodies will be effective partners with local authorities and others in delivering early help.

Supporting partnership working takes resources. Local safeguarding children boards (LSCBs) are seen as key in helping to monitor and performance manage the delivery of early help. How are they to do this without adequate resources? The resourcing of LSCBs has always been problematic, with debate since their creation about what the level of prescription should be for contributing agencies. There is minimal prescription and the result is LSCBs struggling to fulfil their current role, which has expanded since their creation in 2006. They have to find resources for independent chairs and increased requirements for independence in serious case reviews (SCRs). These include independent chairs of SCR panels and independent authors of overview reports, child death review panels and lay members. Will the police, local authorities and NHS commissioners, the key funders of LSCBs, find further funding to support an expanded role in early help in the current financial climate? The absence of a statutory duty will make increased contributions less likely.

Third, how good are we at implementing evidence-based interventions? The conclusion must be that this remains a significant weakness across all key children's agencies. There are problems with the evidence base. It is often hard to find good studies of interventions in the area of safeguarding and child protection. Where there are good studies and related intervention programmes, their take-up across the system is slow. For example, MST has been well tried and researched in the US and MST programmes have been running in the UK for over eight years with good results. Yet take-up is poor and government support has been increased for local authorities and partners using this approach. The same could be said for some other well-known programmes such as Triple P Parenting and aspects of the Sure Start programme.

The Sure Start programme was very thoroughly researched, although there was only one small study focusing on child protection. Yet there is little sense in the revised guidance for Sure Start currently being produced or in discussion of how the programme needs to change of what that evidence base can tell us about effectiveness and impact.

My view is that if we are to deliver better early help, we need a significantly more rigorous focus on delivering evidence-based services. This will require a tougher approach to decommissioning services that do not evidence the positive difference they make and more work on how we measure impact. This is an area where the voluntary and independent sectors could significantly enhance their role by developing, piloting and rigorously evaluating interventions and marketing them to statutory agencies as a means to improve impact and reduce costs in the medium to long term.

Many local authorities and their partners have begun to develop the use of the outcomes-based accountability (OBA) framework as a way to improve their measurement of impact (C4EO, 2010). This approach has the central virtue of getting everyone focused on the 'What difference did we make?' questions and away from measuring inputs, activity and the opinions of service providers on the benefits of their work.

Fourth, we need to develop our workforce and enable it to deliver effective early help to address the child or young person's and the family's needs. The Munro Review and the reports of the Social Work Reform Board (2010) highlight the deficits and development needs of the social work sector of the workforce. There are also significant deficits in other key parts. We have shortages of health visitors and midwives in many regions. It is far from clear how the ambitions of the reforms relating to health visitors, central to the delivery of the Healthy Child Programme, can be met by 2015. Similarly, it is not clear where the staff needed to fill the jobs created by an expanded Family Nurse Partnership programme will come from. In the police force, the requirements to make severe budget reductions are leading to the retirement of many of the most experienced officers and restrictions on recruitment of new officers. Experience counts in all areas of policing but is at a particular premium in safeguarding, child protection and public protection work more generally.

In schools, the focus is on teaching and leadership skills. How far schools will feel able to invest in the skills that support staff to provide early help must be in question. Those schools with the most children in need of early help are likely to be those facing the greatest pressure to meet floor targets for attainment and progress. This conjunction of pressures will severely test the leadership skills of heads and their senior teams as they balance the pressures to raise standards and provide early help and contribute to multi-agency and multidisciplinary working. The trick will be to ensure that the provision of early help addresses barriers to learning and is seen in the medium to long term to contribute to raising attainment and progress.

Social work and social workers remain central to making early help work. Balancing social work resources to early help with remedial interventions to protect children, including removal from home, is very difficult for many local authorities. In many, the social workers working in referral and assessment teams, in neighbourhood teams doing child in need and child protection work, and in many looked-after children teams are relatively inexperienced. It is not unusual for 20 to 40% of staff in these frontline teams to be in their first year or two of practice after qualification. This is not a firm base from which to offer advice to practitioners in partner agencies on the management of risk. Nor is it the best starting point for a programme to free up professional staff from a prescriptive framework of guidance. For many staff and their managers, the guidance is a key tool that enables a basic level of consistency and competence in response to vulnerable children, young people and families to be provided.

If we are to improve the provision of early help and the quality of service to those who need a child protection intervention, then remedying the relative inexperience of the workforce is vital. This will take time. There is a wide consensus that the programme of reform that the Social Work Reform Board is putting in place is right and that, given will and resources, it can deliver the change in the quality and quantity of the workforce required. It is so long since we have had a stable, experienced and well-trained social work workforce in children's services working with manageable caseloads – if we ever did have – we do not know what could be achieved in that situation.

One important component of a revitalised social work profession, which could make a critical difference to the ambition to provide more early help as well as raise standards for child protection services and services for children in care, is the role of the social worker as leader. The role has long included the idea of being a key worker and this is described in the *Working together* guidance (HMG, 2010) in relation to social workers' responsibilities where they are the allocated worker to a child or young person with a child protection plan. However, there has been little description of the role as leader, as opposed to someone who coordinates effort. A leader has a role which includes shaping, directing and motivating the actions of others. This means leading the work with children and young people and their families and other professionals working with the families. Seeing social workers as leaders presents the role as a more powerful change agent in the system. The current bureaucratisation of the social work role and the roles of others who help children and young people does not encourage leadership, which inherently involves acting with autonomy and a sense of one's own agency.

Delivering early help requires leadership from social workers and from their professional partners. I have discussed the leadership role of social workers, but if early help is to work, we will require more professionals to act with leadership and a sense of their own agency to help lead children, young people and families in solving their problems and changing their lives for the better.

Conclusion

In conclusion, the prospects for delivering the recommendations for early help as envisaged by the Munro Review do not look promising. The history of early intervention efforts over the past decade does not suggest that we yet have the experience of success in ensuring that early help makes a difference, which would help make a reality of this recommendation. This was in a period of increasing resources and many initiatives designed to make early help a reality. Some hard reflection is needed on why we have not done better as individual agencies and collectively as a multi-agency and multidisciplinary system charged with improving children's lives.

More positively, there is a great deal to learn about what has and has not worked from recent experience, and the pressure to make best use of resources is leading to a sharper look at what makes a difference for children, young people and their families. The recommendation can be made to work but it will take:

- leadership from government, which includes a statutory duty and the right performance management and inspection requirements to back this up;
- leadership from the key partner agencies, which are willing to use the levers at their disposal, and the multi-agency groups best placed to lead this work such as health and wellbeing boards and LSCBs;
- willingness to take resources from universal services to invest in early help;
- rigorous implementation of what we know about what works in terms of best practice for both early help and remedial help and a willingness to decommission and reshape services that do not demonstrate impact and value for money;
- development of a workforce with the leadership and practice skills to work with a sense of its own agency and autonomy to help children, young people and families change their lives.

References

Allen, G. (2011) *Early intervention: The next steps*, London: Department for Work and Pensions.

C4EO (Centre for Excellence in Outcomes) (2010) *Outcomes based accountability (OBA) toolkit*, London: C4EO.

CAFCASS (Child and Family Court Advisory Support Service) (2011) 'August 2011 care statistics', London: CAFCASS.

DfE (Department for Education) (2002–11) 'Sure Start research programme, 2002–2011', London. Available at: www.education.gov.uk/researchandstatistics/research/researchpublications?q=Sure+Start&page=1 (accessed October 2011).

DfE (2010) *Sure Start children's centres statutory guidance*, October, London: DfE.

DfE (2011) *A child-centred system: The government's response to the Munro Review of Child Protection*, London: DfE. Available at: www.education.gov.uk/publications.

DfE and BIS (Department for Business Innovation and Skills) (2011) 'Statistical first release: referrals, assessments and children who were the subject of a child protection plan' (2010/11 Children in Need census, provisional), London: DfE.

DH (Department of Health) (2009) *Healthy Child Programme, 0 to 5 and 5 to 19*, London: DH.

DH (2011a) *Family Nurse Partnership evidence summary* [leaflet], London: FNP National Unit.

DH (2011b) *Health Visitor Implementation Plan 2011–15: A call to action*, London: DH.

Field, F. (2011) *The foundation years: Preventing poor children becoming poor adults*, London: The Stationery Office.

HMG (Her Majesty's Government) (2010) *Working together to safeguard children: A guide to inter-agency working to safeguard and promote the welfare of children*, London: The Stationery Office.

Institute of Education (1999–2008) *Effectiveness of primary schools in England*, London: DfE and Institute of Education.

Marmot, M. (2010) *The Marmot Review: Fair society, healthy lives: A strategic review of health inequalities in England*, London: Marmot Review Team.

Munro, E. (2011) *The Munro Review of Child Protection: Final report: A child-centred system*, London: DfE. Available at: www.education.gov.uk/publications.

Ofsted (2011) *Inspection 2012: proposals for inspection arrangements for maintained schools and academies from January 2012*, London: Ofsted.

OECD (Organisation for Economic Cooperation and Development) (2011) *Society at a glance*, Paris: OECD.

Social Work Reform Board (2010) *Social Work Reform Board: One year on report*, London: DH.

Tickell, C. (2011) *The early years: Foundations for life, health and learning*, London: DfE.

TWO

Local safeguarding children boards: faith, hope and evidence

Michael Preston-Shoot

Introduction

Since their creation for England and Wales in the 2004 Children Act, local safeguarding children boards (LSCBs) have been invested with hope by policymakers and inquiries. Government ministers have expressed optimism about the potential of LSCBs to make a difference in promoting accountability for practice, generating learning from practice, and monitoring the effectiveness of work with children and their families (DfES, 2007; DfE, 2011).

This faith has been reinforced by inquiries. Laming (2009) recommended strengthening LSCBs through clarifying their relationship with, and distinctiveness from, children's trusts, improving scrutiny and challenge through the production of annual reports and the introduction of greater independence for serious case review (SCR) panel chairs and overview report writers, and by the attendance of senior decision-makers. Munro (2011a, 2011b) does not disturb this trend. She regards LSCBs as uniquely placed to take a holistic approach to child protection, a role she argues is even more important in a tight fiscal climate. She argues that LSCBs have a key role in promoting and supporting learning, identifying and challenging poor practice, monitoring outcomes, and advising on service development to reduce gaps and duplication in provision.

Researchers too have endorsed mechanisms, such as LSCBs and children's trusts, for facilitating interagency cooperation and developing mutual and collective accountability in respect of safeguarding children (O'Brien et al, 2006). This calm is, however, occasionally disturbed by more critical perspectives (Parton, 2006; Chief Inspectors, 2008; Watson, 2010), raising the spectre that LSCBs might be active without contributing much to child protection and children's safeguarding more broadly. They are viewed as adding to unnecessary bureaucracy, duplicating the roles and responsibilities of other collaborative mechanisms, such as children's trusts, and thereby consuming expensive staff and financial resources. Doubts are expressed about their capacity for generating positive outcomes for children and families.

So is this faith and hope justified? Have LSCBs promoted positive outcomes and enhanced explanatory and responsive accountability (Leat, 1996) for the work of safeguarding children? Do they have sufficient statutory and positional authority to do so? Have they facilitated professionals and organisations working together, strategically and operationally, and do they have sufficient reach in terms of resources to do this? Are LSCBs merely adding another edifice to an overcrowded architectural jungle or are they an essential element in safeguarding and promoting the welfare of children and their families and communities? Can LSCBs be (part of) the difference that makes a difference, mindful of the history of attempts since the death of Maria Colwell to construct a system that will effectively protect children?

This chapter will examine the position and role of LSCBs in a changing and challenging policy landscape. It will review the research evidence and draw on personal experience of being an independent chair of one LSCB.

Mandate

LSCBs were created by the 2004 Children Act.[1] Section 13 requires each local authority to establish an LSCB with representatives drawn as a minimum from the police, probation, youth offending teams (YOTs), strategic health authorities (SHAs), NHS trusts and primary care trusts (PCTs), CAFCASS, prisons and secure training centres. Two or more local authorities may combine when establishing their LSCBs. Section 14 specifies that LSCB functions are to coordinate work to safeguard and promote children's welfare, and to ensure its

effectiveness. Section 15 permits partners to make payments or offer resources towards expenditure. Section 16 empowers the Secretary of State to issue guidance, which LSCBs must follow.

The 2006 Local Safeguarding Children Boards Regulations and the 2006 Local Safeguarding Children Boards (Wales) Regulations elaborate on the duties outlined in the 2004 Children Act. Each LSCB must have at least one representative of the local authority and each of its partners, all with sufficient seniority. Each authority must consult partners and then appoint a chairperson. LSCB functions are detailed as follows:

- to develop, audit and challenge policies and procedures for safeguarding and promoting the welfare of children;
- to raise awareness of how individuals and organisations can safeguard and promote the welfare of children;
- to monitor and evaluate effectiveness of how the authority and partners individually and collectively safeguard and promote children's welfare and advise on improvements;
- to participate in service planning;
- to listen to children, young people and their families and to draw on their insights when engaged in their other functions;
- to review serious cases (where abuse or neglect is known or suspected and where a child has died or been seriously harmed and there is cause for concern about how agencies worked together) and advise on lessons to be learned;
- to collect and analyse information about child deaths, putting in place procedures for ensuring a coordinated public health and safety response.

Statutory guidance (Welsh Government Guidance, 2006; DfE, 2010) added further detail. An LSCB core responsibility is the effective coordination of agencies to secure prevention and protection, and subsequently to enhance the five statutory outcomes for children outlined in the 2004 Children Act. Core functions include: developing thresholds, policies and procedures; communication and awareness raising; monitoring and evaluation; and overseeing child death reviews and SCRs.

The same guidance lists LSCB activities. These include responsibility for:

- prevention: safer recruitment, organisational audits to ensure that all agencies working with children take account of the need to safeguard and promote their welfare, publicising contact points, using key performance indicators, conducting public campaigns;
- targeting: setting thresholds and procedures for children in need and for vulnerable groups – disabled children, gangs, private fostering, youth justice;
- responding to harm: overseeing thresholds for section 47 (1989 Children Act) investigations; developing or facilitating the development of agreed protocols and procedures for joint investigations, forced marriage, multi-agency assessments, parents with mental illness, trafficked children, domestic violence, cross-border working and the transition point between children's and adult services for care leavers and disabled young people;
- planning and commissioning: consulting young people, scrutinising the plans of the children's trust or, in Wales, the children and young people's partnership;
- monitoring, evaluating and auditing, and advising agencies on how to improve services: how safe are employment practices? Are thresholds commonly understood? Are referrals appropriate? Are children's life chances improved? This involves self- and peer assessment, case file audits and investigations of serious incidents. LSCBs may challenge agencies on actions (not) taken for improvement.

LSCBs may cooperate with neighbouring authorities and should have procedures for handling complaints and resolving differences between agencies. They must promote equality of opportunity but are not accountable for the operational work of individual agencies. They may engage directly in the provision of interagency training and must set priorities for and then evaluate the quality of intra- and interagency training.

On structures, the same statutory guidance presumes that LSCBs will have independent chairs to ensure effective challenge. Members

will hold key strategic roles for safeguarding, be able to commit their agencies on policy and practice and hold their organisations accountable. Core members will be drawn from the police, SHAs, PCTs, NHS trusts, probation, CAFCASS, YOTs, schools/FE **[in full?]** colleges, and children's social care. It is also advised that members are drawn from the NSPCC, faith groups, children's centres, GPs, voluntary organisations, and the United Kingdom Border Agency (UKBA). Other agencies should be involved when occasion demands, including the Crown Prosecution Service, drug action and alcohol teams, domestic violence forums, and service users. The police, PCT and local authority should contribute resources, the volume to be agreed locally, usually via a pooled budget, to secure staffing for the effective performance of LSCB functions. Members' roles on the LSCB should take precedence over their roles as representatives of their own organisations. The LSCB may create an executive and subgroups. The director of children's services (DCS) is accountable to the council's chief executive for LSCB performance. Elected members have a governance oversight role, with the lead member an LSCB participant observer.

LSCBs have acquired additional statutory duties. The 2009 Apprenticeships, Skills, Children and Learning Act requires them to have two lay members (section 196) and to publish an annual report (section 197). The 2010 Children, Schools and Families Act enables LSCBs to request information from individuals and/or agencies who must comply if the request is relevant to the board's functions and they hold the information. The 2010 Local Safeguarding Children Boards (Amendment) Regulations require that schools and FE colleges are represented on each LSCB.

Evidence

Area child protection committees (ACPCs), the forerunners of LSCBs, were criticised for lacking effective statutory authority, for having insufficient resources and for being ineffective because of variable membership and unclear operational structures (France et al, 2009; Horwath, 2010). Research evidence on which to judge whether arrangements for LSCBs and their performance represent an improvement is neither extensive nor uniformly positive, leading Morrison (2010) to conclude that little is currently known about the workings of such strategic partnerships and their outcomes.

An early review (DfES, 2007), perhaps understandably, found variable progress. Generally, statutory partners had been engaged, although with little SHA involvement. Concerns were articulated about resources, with discussions about budgets seen as distracting LSCBs from their main functions and responsibilities. Engagement with children and families and mechanisms through which boards could review their own performance were underdeveloped.

Another early review (Healthcare Commission, 2007) found that the transition from ACPCs to LSCBs had significantly improved the level of seniority of involvement from NHS trusts and the scrutiny of compliance to safeguarding standards. However, it expressed concerns about the attendance of NHS staff on training courses, about evidence that some healthcare professionals were not following basic child protection procedures, and about levels of partnership working to improve the health and wellbeing of the most vulnerable children.

These themes were echoed in a subsequent review (Chief Inspectors, 2008). Boards were positively evaluated for showing greater independence in chairing and reporting arrangements, and for adopting a wider safeguarding role. However, not all statutory partners, whose engagement is required by law, had become fully involved, with the spotlight falling especially on NHS trusts and PCTs. Insufficient priority had been given by LSCBs to some groups of children, particularly those in private fostering or unaccompanied and seeking asylum. The review found wide variation in the attendance of non-statutory partners and in decision-making about whether to commission SCRs. Consultation with children and young people remained underdeveloped. Concerns were expressed about the monitoring of agency compliance with safer recruitment and about whether practitioners had sufficient knowledge of child protection. The review concluded that LSCBs were not yet in a position to demonstrate the impact of their work.

Gardner and Brandon (2008) reached similar conclusions. While positive use had been made of the work of LSCBs, for instance by some NHS trusts in developing their safeguarding focus, boards were inadequately resourced. Moreover, some professionals or organisations, such as GPs and child and adolescent mental health services, had refused to engage, either in a board's work or in child protection training.

On specific LSCB functions, some positive evidence has emerged. Boards have led or facilitated the development of innovative practice, for instance around domestic violence protocols (Stanley et al, 2011) and engagement with faith communities (Rao and Rao, 2010). They have provided positive drive and established good working relationships with respect to reviewing and learning from child deaths (Sidebotham et al, 2008). There are good examples of effective interagency training (Carpenter et al, 2010).

One wide-ranging review of LSCBs in England also reported a mixed performance picture (France et al, 2009, 2010). On the positive side, the researchers found that structures were generally in place to enable boards to function effectively, such as the appointment of business managers, the creation of executives and subgroups, and the production of terms of reference and membership protocols. On *focus*, boards were more effective where they had determined main priorities which were realistic rather than where they had adopted an ambitiously broad remit. On *governance*, there was evidence of strong leadership from LSCB chairs and in most cases those attending had sufficient seniority to speak for, commit and hold their agency accountable. On *multi-agency working*, the researchers found progress in the development of a shared vision and language and an improvement in the information available for staff to support their work.

More critically, the researchers found that LSCBs were struggling to carry out their statutory duties, such as communicating with the public, due to resource constraints. Suggestive of weakness in their *statutory mandate*, just over half of board chairs reported difficulties securing funds and having to subsist on inadequate budgets. On *quality*, reported challenges included the cost, in terms of time and finance, and the quality of individual management reviews and overview reports for SCRs. On *communication*, boards appeared to struggle to find effective mechanisms for disseminating and embedding learning in frontline practice and engaging with children, young people and their communities, indicative perhaps of the challenge of *distance*.

On *focus*, LSCBs struggled with ambiguity over their role and function, with differences of opinion concerning whether they should embrace a wider safeguarding agenda or concentrate on child protection. Some boards clearly had difficulty sustaining a wider safeguarding focus. On *governance* and *accountability*, there were tensions between focusing on strategic or operational concerns, and difficulties resolving strong lines of accountability between LSCB chairs, directors of children's services, council chief executives and lead members. For around one quarter of boards, the distinction between their roles and responsibilities and those of children's trusts was reported to be unclear, with the researchers concluding that mutual accountability between the two bodies was problematic.

On *partnership* working, the researchers concluded that some LSCBs had difficulty maintaining continuity of membership and regular attendance at board and subgroup meetings. Just under half of all boards had still been unable to engage all statutory partners, such as PCTs, and other recommended members such as GPs, third sector organisations and faith groups. The Care Quality Commission (CQC) (2009) has observed that the challenge is not just to secure attendance but also to engage all agencies in the effective oversight of safeguarding children. In such instances, LSCBs' *authority* was compromised by lack of clarity about the implications of non-compliance with statutory guidance by partners.

Their final judgement was that LSCBs had been able to address the weaknesses of ACPCs but that they were only performing at 65% effectiveness (France et al, 2010).

Similar themes emerged from a review in Wales of LSCBs (National Assembly for Wales Health, Wellbeing and Local Government Committee, 2010). Boards had made variable progress concerning the discharge of their statutory functions and no clear relationship was found between their effectiveness and the quality of safeguarding children's services. There was a lack of consistency in the commissioning of SCRs and dissatisfaction sometimes with the learning derived from them. Weaknesses were identified in joint working between boards and other partnership bodies, and in funding arrangements, leading to concerns about resources. Problems with information sharing across agencies remained. Practitioners were insufficiently aware of board responsibilities and young people were often unable to participate meaningfully.

Finally, Ofsted (2011) has published a review with examples of where LSCBs have demonstrated good practice with respect to governance, quality assurance, learning from practice, and engaging frontline staff, young people and communities. However, it admits that there are still issues with which even the best boards struggle and that it remains difficult to evidence impact on the outcomes for children and families.

Challenges

Scrutiny of the legal mandate and the effectiveness evidence identifies key challenges for LSCBs. Arguably, there has been greater recognition in Wales than in England by policy makers of the challenges facing boards.

Context

Driscoll (2009) questions whether the scale of the challenge of improving child protection systems and practice has been fully appreciated. Several features of the context in which practice, and the management, regulation and governance of practice, takes place make transformational change difficult to achieve. These features include: high service thresholds and preoccupation with eligibility criteria and resources; weaknesses in the legal mandate, especially the vulnerability of duties relating to children in need (Children Act 1989, s 17) to resource constraint and child protection workloads; and staffing levels in health and social care services, which are inadequate compared to the needs presented.

One aspect of the challenge of context, then, is the work environment in which practice is located. Laming (2009) draws attention to low morale, poor supervision and high caseloads. Welbourne (2010) highlights inexperience among frontline staff. Brooks and Brocklehurst (2010) point to the significant increase in safeguarding activity and the evidence that growth in social work, health visiting and specialist police officer teams has been insufficient to meet the additional demand. Charles and Horwath (2009) focus on staff turnover, which, alongside demanding workloads, makes it difficult for agencies to release staff for training. Dudau (2009) demonstrates how leadership on safeguarding can be inhibited by the capacities within organisations, the people who represent those agencies at LSCB level, and the detailed public scrutiny given to child protection.

A second aspect of context is the proliferation of rules, protocols and targets generated in an attempt to manage risk (Stanley, 2010). Munro (2011a) emphasises how professionals have become constrained by the demands and rigidity of present child protection systems, and how compliance with procedures has become the quality benchmark rather than a focus on learning. Other researchers have also argued that managerialism, characterised by rules, regulations, procedures, targets and audit, has drawn attention away from the core of effective safeguarding work, including relationship building, legal and ethical literacy, informed innovation, reflection, and emotional support for practitioners (Dudau, 2009; Ferguson, 2009; Social Work Task Force, 2009; Ayre and Preston-Shoot, 2010). It is little surprise, then, that inquiries, judicial reviews, ombudsman reports and research find that health and social care professionals and agencies do not always follow good practice, basic child protection procedures and legal rules, or that the rights, voices, needs and wellbeing of children and families are sometimes overlooked (Healthcare Commission, 2007; Chief Inspectors, 2008; Preston-Shoot, 2010; Munro, 2011b).

A third aspect of context is the observation that the organisations involved in safeguarding have different priorities and professional boundaries (Audit Commission, 2008; Ofsted, 2009) and diverse cultures. That information sharing remains difficult to ensure in practice (France et al, 2010), notwithstanding legislation (Data Protection Act 1998) and guidance (DH, 2000) which outline when information should be shared, illustrates the challenge to multi-agency collaborative activity presented by professional education, territoriality, language, ethos, local procedures, status and mandates. All these enter the LSCB arena and have to be managed. Another indication of competing imperatives is that not all statutory partners are fully involved (Gardner and Brandon, 2008; Charles and Horwath, 2009) or willing to commit resources (Dudau, 2009).

One challenge for LSCBs, given their mandate, is whether they can step sufficiently outside this context to act effectively on it. Another is whether boards have sufficient expertise, commitment and positional authority to bridge organisational diversity and separateness. Can senior managers forge strong alliances to encourage the development of trust and challenge in respect of strategic safeguarding developments and operational frontline delivery (Gardner and Brandon, 2008)?

Challenging

A key role for LSCBs involves holding individual agencies and the community of organisations involved in safeguarding children accountable. Early and continuing evidence suggests that this is itself challenging. Questions have been asked about:

- whether there is sufficient challenge in SCR panels (Ofsted, 2008);
- whether current accountability arrangements, including reporting lines to other partnership bodies and elected members, and situations where chairs are not independent of the agencies represented around the table, compromise a board's ability to challenge (DfES, 2007);
- whether agencies are sufficiently rigorous in identifying their own areas of weakness and in challenging others (Driscoll, 2009; Welbourne, 2010);
- whether the size of LSCBs and the time available assist or block levels of participation (France et al, 2010).

The development of peer review, sector-led improvement support and case audit systems, increased reporting to scrutiny committees, and the independence of the LSCB chair may bring a sense of objectivity and challenge, especially when a climate of trust can be created which promotes openness (Ofsted, 2011). However, further evidence is needed to test the outcomes of these potential facilitators.

Distance

There are several components in the challenge of distance. One is between LSCBs and senior management. An illustration emerges from an investigation of cases of professional abuse (ESTYN and CSSIW, 2011), none of which had been reported to the LSCB. This meant that the board had not been able to consider whether to commission SCRs. The investigation concluded that the local authority had not done enough to ensure that the board was well informed about safeguarding issues and, indeed, that senior executives themselves had given insufficient routine attention to this priority. The board had not received regular reports to enable it to make an independent evaluation of strategic and operational safeguarding practice. Managers may have minimised safeguarding concerns and the board may not have had the confidence in its governance role or authority to challenge.

This investigation is less critical of how active or effective the LSCB was, or should have been, in examining the absence of routine reporting. However, other reports on breakdowns in patient safety and care in the NHS and in social care have highlighted what can happen when governing bodies rely on and are insufficiently challenging of senior managers (for example, CSCI and Healthcare Commission, 2006; Cantrill et al, 2010; Francis, 2010).

A second component is the distance between LSCBs and bodies which might scrutinise their functioning and effectiveness. The aforementioned investigation into professional abuse found that the board did not report to the local overview and scrutiny committee and additionally that elected members were not briefed by senior managers, with the result that issues were masked and those with some authority to hold agency leaders accountable were unsighted on safeguarding issues. Scrutiny committees might also query whether board chairs and senior managers would openly admit to difficulties when questioned.

Concerns have also been expressed about whether independent chairs have difficulty bridging the gap between their role on the board and the wider partnership architecture that shares responsibility for safeguarding children (France et al, 2010; National Assembly for Wales Health, Wellbeing and Local Government Committee, 2010).

Finally, the distance between LSCBs and operational staff, children and young people, and local communities has been highlighted (for example, National Assembly for Wales Health, Wellbeing and Local Government Committee, 2010). Good practice has been commended, for instance in the shape of practitioner groups, business days, annual conferences, community safety initiatives and public awareness campaigns, user participation groups, and engagement with young people's groups and faith groups (Sidebotham et al, 2008; Burke, 2010; France et al, 2010; Rao and Rao, 2010; Ofsted, 2011). Morrison (2010), for instance, talks about the importance of engaging with practitioner narratives so that boards know what is really happening and, using this knowledge, can address systemic problems and support frontline staff to learn and improve the quality of practice. However, the question remains whether LSCBs have sufficient time, funding, knowledge and expertise to overcome these illustrations of distance. One report (National Assembly for Wales Health, Wellbeing and Local Government Committee, 2010) has recommended that further guidance is needed on the involvement of children and young people.

Authority

The challenge of engaging some professional groups in training, and in safeguarding generally (CQC, 2009; Carpenter et al, 2010), draws attention to the mandate. The challenge of authority emerges from this mandate and the resources with which boards can generate capacity and capability.

On the specific mandate in the legal rules, LSCBs have neither powers nor sanctions to require partner agencies to make financial contributions or to participate in board activities, including joint training. They have responsibility for providing positional leadership but possess limited powers to support the discharge of their statutory functions in relation to the development and scrutiny of multi-agency safeguarding policy and practice locally (Dudau, 2009; Horwath,

2010; National Assembly for Wales Health, Wellbeing and Local Government Committee, 2010).

Additionally, the legal mandate which more broadly underpins and reinforces partnership working can be criticised. It enables rather than requires agencies, such as children's social care, to request collaboration with respect to individual cases, with other agencies having the discretion to determine whether the request is reasonable. It focuses largely on bringing diverse organisations into dialogue on individual cases rather than promoting organisational integration at operational levels. Practitioners and managers may not find it easy to understand and/or implement the powers and duties available to them, for instance with respect to requesting information (Preston-Shoot, 2009).

The mandate that establishes LSCBs has constructed and superimposed a multi-agency structure on a field otherwise largely comprising individual, discrete organisations. There are two critical facets here. First, despite the 2004 Children Act focus on outcomes for children, organisational and professional cultures have been left largely untouched and the interface with other legal powers and duties, such as those contained in the 1989 Children Act with respect to children in need and children requiring protection, left unexplained. Thus there remains a continuing preoccupation with individual cases, with insufficient focus and resources invested in developing the capacity of communities to make further contributions to safeguarding and outcomes for children (Jack, 2006).

Second, the mandate is arguably weak in helping boards integrate safeguarding activity within and across partner agencies. Arrangements for working together may lie along a continuum (Dudau and McAllister, 2010; Horwath, 2010). At one end is case cooperation, where agencies communicate and share information but retain their autonomy. Moving along the continuum, there may be greater cooperation on strategic planning and intervention with children, families and their communities, but organisational identity is retained. Further along, agencies may commit to a common mission and a duty to cooperate, which involves some loss of autonomy. At the other end, agencies may become highly integrated. LSCBs fall somewhere around the midpoint of the continuum. They are heavily reliant on the willingness of partners to align activities, operations and cultures to a common goal, where one challenge may be to surmount long-established professional and organisational cultures, and on the capacity of members to provide high-quality leadership that consistently brings agencies back to partnership values and collaborative capacity building (Dudau, 2009; Dudau and McAllister, 2010; Horwath, 2010).

Alongside observations regarding the mandate sit questions about capacity. Concerns about the adequacy of resources, with which boards can invest strategically in safeguarding activity, emerge routinely from research (DfES, 2007; France et al, 2009; Carpenter et al, 2010; National Assembly for Wales Health, Wellbeing and Local Government Committee, 2010). Capacity depends not just on finance but on resources more broadly, including time, understanding and skills with which to evaluate the outcomes of joint training, engage with faith communities, address the economic wellbeing of children and young people, or create learning organisations, for example.

Neither Munro (2011b) nor Ofsted (2011) address these systemic weaknesses, which are a continuation from previous ACPC arrangements. Equally, criticisms have been voiced that regulators underestimate the extent and depth of the difficulties faced by LSCBs (Gardner and Brandon, 2008). However, they have been recognised to some degree in Wales (National Assembly for Wales Health, Wellbeing and Local Government Committee, 2010). Several committee recommendations are pertinent here. One advises the Welsh government to strengthen the duty to cooperate and consider whether current LSCB powers are sufficiently robust. Another focuses on the legal rules surrounding partnership working more generally and recommends revised guidance on information sharing and the duties of partner agencies. A third recommends that guidance on agency contributions should be strengthened so that statutory partners must contribute.

Focus

Safeguarding, whether of children or of adults, is sometimes perceived as an ambiguous concept or an elastic term (Parton, 2006; Braye et al, 2011). Some have welcomed this widening role (Chief Inspectors, 2008). Others have questioned whether LSCBs can or indeed should focus on the needs of all children or whether they are better advised to focus on child protection (O'Brien et al, 2006; DfES, 2007; Franceet al, 2009). In Wales, boards are required to focus on child protection and engage with wider remits when this appears secure (National Assembly for Wales Health, Wellbeing and Local Government Committee, 2010). Either way, the potential scope of safeguarding activity is considerable, such that Ofsted (2011) has advised LSCBs to focus on a limited number of priorities, derived from local and national learning and regularly reviewed.

If one aspect of this continuum along which LSCBs settle runs between child protection and wider safeguarding functions and outcomes, another differentiates between proactive and reactive activity. The former includes active monitoring of specific groups of children, such as those with specific needs, and awareness raising among staff, alongside routine appraisal of staffing resources and capabilities and the health of the organisational context, reflected in supervision, staff capacity and workloads (Rose and Barnes, 2008; Social Work Task Force, 2009). The latter includes acting on learning from the outcomes of particular cases.

A second continuum captures an early concern that LSCBs may default to a focus on operational matters rather than holding a strategic role (DfES, 2007). Stanley (2010) suggests that boards indeed have a dual focus – scrutinising the strategic management of child protection while also looking at the realities of practice. Munro (2011a, 2011b) advocates strengthening of the LSCBs' role in monitoring the impact of practice and training on the child's journey, and identifying and addressing emerging problems. She refers in particular to focusing on children's participation, the quality of relationships established with children and families, and the effectiveness of intervention and support given to frontline staff. Gardner and Brandon (2008) and Morrison (2010) argue that LSCBs should devote time and resources to listening and responding to frontline needs, which implies engagement with operational concerns and scrutiny of how senior managers individually and collectively address workforce development strategically (Charles and Horwath, 2009).

A third continuum describes how LSCBs balance an individual with a community focus. Jack and Gill (2010) capture this vividly by presenting research evidence that demonstrates the impact of a child's wider circumstances on their wellbeing and then noting that the role of community factors in children's wellbeing is insufficiently acknowledged in statutory guidance on assessment, protection and multi-agency collaboration. They observe that different communities will possibly perceive safeguarding and outcomes for children differently and urge boards to listen to children, families and communities, to support the safeguarding activities of local people and to promote partnership approaches to extending local provision. Munro (2011b) also recommends that LSCBs, when monitoring and evaluating multi-agency safeguarding activity, take account of local need and the effectiveness of help. She also advocates a holistic approach to child protection, which implies a focus wider than individual families. However, she does not address the dominant individual case orientation of healthcare agencies and children's services (Jack, 2006) in her recommendations, thereby missing an opportunity to refocus on community development.

A fourth continuum distinguishes between process and task. Process focuses on the impact of professional roles, including power and status differences, the nature and quality of interactions and relationships between board members and the organisations they represent, the experiences and narratives that people have individually and collectively about working together, and the development of capacity by, *inter alia*, making explicit the values, knowledge and skills that people bring and harnessing this resource into partnership working. It refers to the challenge of facilitating members to rise above their everyday roles and preoccupations. Task refers to determining where each LSCB decides to focus and how the statutory functions of individual protection and planning, specific initiatives to address the need of particular groups, community awareness raising and specific initiatives are weighed in the balance and taken forward.

Finally, there is the tension between managing compliance with statutory guidance, with a focus on audit and monitoring, and leading practice and the management of practice. That involves, at least, the encouragement of individual and collective learning through recognition of the certainty of uncertainty in child protection, provision of environments where anxiety and not knowing can be contained, and appreciative conversations with practitioners, managers and researchers (Morrison, 2010).

Governance

Reports have identified the difficulties that LSCBs have encountered with developing or maintaining governance arrangements, and with separating executive from scrutiny functions (CQC, 2009; France et al, 2010; National Assembly for Wales Health, Wellbeing and Local Government Committee, 2010; ESTYN and CSSIW, 2011). The focus has fallen on poorly developed audit systems, tardiness in pressing for action or challenging the lack of information about serious incidents or compliance with care standards, and low priority accorded to appraisal and development of board members.

Clear lines of accountability are required (National Assembly for Wales Health, Wellbeing and Local Government Committee, 2010; Munro, 2011b), so attention has been given to LSCBs giving account to and holding other partnership bodies and individual agencies to account through routine and annual reports. However, the complexities of accountability have, arguably, been underestimated. Less attention has been given to how independent chairs and boards might hold senior executives to account for acts or omissions when agency and multi-agency structures are either unfamiliar or closed to them. Indeed, problems have arisen when senior managers have been unwilling to engage in monitoring safeguarding policy and practice (France et al, 2010; ESTYN and CSSIW, 2011). Similarly, boards have to negotiate both vertical (within individual agencies) and horizontal (across agencies) accountability. This may involve proactive accountability in the setting of standards and reactive accountability when boards call agencies to account for their performance (Leat, 1996).

Guidance on governance draws attention to particular layers (Audit Commission, 2005, 2008; Sidebotham et al, 2008; France et al, 2010; Horwath, 2010; OPSI, 2010; Ofsted, 2011). It highlights the importance of:

- Agreeing strategic direction, or purpose and outcomes. This includes statements of core values, desired outputs and outcomes, translated into clear priorities and plans.
- Establishing effective structures, which include decisions on member roles and responsibilities, chairing arrangements, lines of accountability and agreements on how performance of the board and of agencies will be measured. The focus here is on how decisions are made, on functions and protocols, and on planning and reviewing mechanisms so that LSCBs can adapt to change. Structures need to facilitate planning and the engagement of service users, communities and frontline staff, as well as being capable of assuring quality and measuring impact.
- Building capacity for partnership working, scrutiny and challenge, where members bring specialist knowledge of safeguarding and/or of communities, strategic and communication skills, and the positional authority to secure change in their organisations. Resources are adequate to enable investment in service improvement. Membership is stable and confident, underpinned by sound induction and appraisal systems, so that understanding of roles and responsibilities is secure. When members represent individual agencies and when they act as a collective board community is negotiated and agreed. Consideration is given to the balance struck between exclusive membership, where a shared understanding and focus may be more easily developed but at the possible expense of links beyond the board, and inclusive membership, where a large group brings experience and expertise but at the potential cost of keeping focus and maintaining open communication.
- Developing a culture based on trusting relationships and engagement with service users, communities and staff, which informs the board's work. Communication is open and a shared language develops. Leadership is strong. Members are able and willing to transcend the professional roles and identities that they initially bring to the board.

Quality

To strengthen their impact, LSCBs should investigate the effectiveness of help provided to children and families, use performance information more intelligently and evaluate not just whether practice is good or unacceptable but what may be learned from it (Munro, 2011b). Other researchers have also urged more rigorous evaluation and the triangulation of findings, with evidence from children and young people and from research (Charles and Horwath, 2009; Carpenter et al, 2010).

However, not all boards are receiving routine performance reports, and where they do, the focus is often on quantitative data and on children's social care rather than the whole safeguarding system (Brooks and Brocklehurst, 2010; National Assembly for Wales Health, Wellbeing and Local Government Committee, 2010). Equally, while the quality of SCRs has improved, more evidence is needed of whether recommended actions have been implemented and improved the quality of child protection (Rose and Barnes, 2008; Ofsted, 2009).

Suggestions have been offered for effective ways of gathering data to ensure quality, including methodologies to evaluate the outcomes of training (Carpenter et al, 2010) and the use of case reviews, thematic audits, peer reviews, peer challenge and learning sets to monitor, learn from and adapt practice (LGG et al, 2011; Munro, 2011b; Ofsted, 2011). Whether boards are appropriately resourced to engage fully with this activity is a moot point, especially when the list of recommended areas for quality assurance (LGID, 2011) is considered. These include key tasks, such as assessment and planning; use of resources; particular vulnerable groups such as disabled children; specific issues such as domestic violence, forced marriage and trafficking; partnership working at operational and strategic levels; engagement with children and families; and organisational culture, including supervision and workloads. This quality activity concludes with single agency reports and/or analysis of cross-cutting themes, leading to action planning and subsequent further reviews.

Meanwhile, some themes continue to emerge routinely from SCRs, such as record keeping, information sharing, recognition of signs and symptoms, communication between professionals, mental health, substance misuse, engagement with children, scrutiny of chronology and review of approaches taken to cases (Rose and Barnes, 2008; Ofsted, 2008, 2009; Brandon et al, 2010). Such repetition suggests that quality reviews need to focus beyond single and multi-agency practice in individual cases to the systemic factors that surround it, including the legal and policy mandate, organisational culture, the assumption that the world of child protection is a rational activity amenable solely to technical solutions, and the dynamics of human networks and interactions.

Conclusion

The complexities of safeguarding children and the mandate given to LSCBs have, arguably, been underestimated. Munro's recommendations (2011b), while necessary because of the changing partnership architecture in England, are essentially cosmetic, missing an opportunity for critique and a rethinking of mandate, partnership structures and resources. Recommendations from the Welsh review (National Assembly for Wales Health, Wellbeing and Local Government Committee, 2010) are more far-reaching but may also prove insufficient to address the formidable array of challenges facing LSCBs.

Recommendations in the Munro (2011b) and Social Work Task Force (2009) reports, which seek to reinforce employers' obligations towards frontline staff, provide career structures for social workers, enhance the use of social work expertise and protect the roles of senior childcare managers, are also necessary but strangely ahistorical. The problems they are designed to address have been a significant feature of the social work landscape for decades. What might ensure progress this time, especially if the report recommendations remain advisory rather than mandatory (Preston-Shoot, 2010)?

Systems create challenges. What LSCBs have achieved is commendable. However, their potential to deliver transformational change is limited by the failure of policymakers to consider how systems that surround them also need to change in order to deliver better outcomes for children.

Note

[1] The sections which follow relate to England. Part 3 of the 2004 Children Act repeats the requirements for Wales, with boards required to ensure that relevant organisations in each local authority area cooperate to safeguard and promote the welfare of children (National Assembly for Wales Health, Wellbeing and Local Government Committee, 2010).

References

Audit Commission (2005) *Governing partnerships: Bridging the accountability gap*, London: Audit Commission.

Audit Commission (2008) *Are we getting there? Improving governance and resource management in children's trusts*, London: Audit Commission.

Ayre, P. and Preston-Shoot, M. (eds) (2010) *Children's services at the crossroads: A critical evaluation of contemporary policy for practice*, Lyme Regis: Russell House Publishing.

Brandon, M., Bailey, S. and Belderson, P. (2010) *Building on the learning from serious case reviews: A two-year analysis of child protection, database notifications 2007–2009*, London: DfE.

Braye, S., Orr, D. and Preston-Shoot, M. (2011) *The governance of adult safeguarding: Findings from research into adult safeguarding boards*, London: SCIE.

Brooks, C. and Brocklehurst, P. (2010) *Safeguarding pressures report, phase 2: Exploring reasons and effect*, London: Association of Directors of Children's Services.

Burke, T. (2010) *Anyone listening? Evidence of children and young people's participation in England*, London: National Children's Bureau.

Cantrill, P., Foster, E., Lane, P. and Pate, R. (2010) *Report of the independent inquiry into the Colin Norris incidents at Leeds Teaching Hospitals NHS Trust in 2002*, Leeds: Yorkshire and the Humber SHA.

Carpenter, J., Hackett, S., Patsios, D. and Szilassy, E. (2010) *Outcomes of inter-agency training to safeguard children: Final report to the Department for Children, Schools and Families and the Department of Health*, London: Department for Children, Schools and Families (DCSF).

Charles, M. and Horwath, J. (2009) 'Investing in interagency training to safeguard children: an act of faith or an act of reason?', *Children and Society*, 23, pp 364–76.

Chief Inspectors (2008) *Safeguarding children: The third joint Chief Inspectors' report on arrangements to safeguard children*, London: The Stationery Office.

CQC (Care Quality Commission) (2009) *Safeguarding children: A review of arrangements in the NHS for safeguarding children*, London: CQC.

CSCI (Commission for Social Care Inspection) and Healthcare Commission (2006) *Joint investigation into the provision of services for people with learning disabilities at Cornwall Partnership NHS Trust*, London: Commission for Healthcare Audit and Inspection.

DfE (Department for Education) (2010) *Working together to safeguard children: A guide to inter-agency working to safeguard and promote the welfare of children*, London: The Stationery Office.

DfE (2011) *A child-centred system: The government's response to the Munro Review of Child Protection*, London: The Stationery Office. Available at: www.education.gov.uk/publications.

DfES (Department for Education and Skills) (2007) *Local safeguarding children boards: A review of progress*, London: DfES.

DH (Department of Health) (2000) *Data Protection Act: Guidance to social services*, London: DH.

Driscoll, J. (2009) 'Prevalence, people and processes: a consideration of the implications of Lord Laming's progress report on the protection of children in England', *Child Abuse Review*, 18, pp 333–45.

Dudau, A. (2009) 'Leadership in public sector partnerships: a case study of local safeguarding children boards', *Public Policy and Administration*, 24, pp 399–415.

Dudau, A. and McAllister, L. (2010) 'Developing collaborative capacities by fostering diversity in organizations: evidence from a case study of youth offending teams in local safeguarding children boards', *Public Management Review*, 12(3), pp 385–402.

ESTYN and CSSIW (2011) *Joint investigation into the handling and management of allegations of professional abuse and the arrangements for safeguarding and protecting children in education services in Pembrokeshire County Council*, Cardiff: The Stationery Office.

Ferguson, H. (2009) 'Performing child protection: home visiting, movement and the struggle to reach the abused child', *Child and Family Social Work*, 14, pp 471–80.

France, A., Munro, E.R., Meredith, J., Manful, E. and Beckhelling, J. (2009) *Effectiveness of the new local safeguarding children boards in England: Interim report*, London: DCSF.

France, A., Munro, E.R. and Waring, A. (2010) *The evaluation of arrangements for effective operation of the new local safeguarding children boards in England: Final report*, London: DfE.

Francis, R. (2010) *Independent inquiry into care provided by Mid Staffordshire NHS Foundation Trust, January 2005–March 2009*, London: The Stationery Office.

Gardner, R. and Brandon, M. (2008) 'Child protection: crisis management or learning curve?', *Public Policy Research*, 15(4), pp 177–86.

Healthcare Commission (2007) *Safeguarding children and young people: A shared responsibility*, London: Commission for Healthcare Audit and Inspection.

Horwath, J. (2010) 'Rearing a toothless tiger? From area child protection committee to local safeguarding children board', *Journal of Children's Services*, 5(3), pp 37–47.

Jack, G. (2006) 'The area and community components of children's well-being', *Children and Society*, 20, pp 334–47.

Jack, G. and Gill, O. (2010) 'The role of communities in safeguarding children', *Child Abuse Review*, 19, pp 82–96.

Laming, H. (2009) *The protection of children in England: A progress report*, London: HMSO.

Leat, D. (1996) 'Are voluntary organisations accountable?', in D. Billis and M. Harris (eds) *Voluntary agencies, challenges of organisation and management*, Basingstoke: Macmillan.

LGG (Local Government Group), Association of Directors of Children's Services and SOLACE (2011) *Towards excellence for children: Sector-led improvement and support in children's services*, London: LGG.

LGID (Local Government Improvement and Development) (2011) *Improving local safeguarding outcomes: Developing a strategic quality assurance framework to safeguard children*, London: LGID.

Morrison, T. (2010) 'The strategic leadership of complex practice: opportunities and challenges', *Child Abuse Review*, 19, pp 312–29.

Munro, E. (2011a) *The Munro Review of Child Protection: Interim report: The child's journey*, London: The Stationery Office. Available at: www.education.gov.uk/publications.

Munro, E. (2011b) *The Munro Review of Child Protection: Final report: A child-centred system*, London: The Stationery Office. Available at: www.education.gov.uk/publications.

National Assembly for Wales Health, Wellbeing and Local Government Committee (2010) *Inquiry into local safeguarding boards in Wales*, Cardiff: Welsh Assembly.

O'Brien, M., Bachman, M., Husbands, C., Shreeve, A., Jones, N., Watson, J. and Shemilt, I. (2006) 'Integrating children's services to promote children's welfare: early findings from the implementation of children's trusts in England', *Child Abuse Review*, 15, pp 377–95.

Ofsted (2008) *Learning lessons, taking action: Ofsted's evaluations of serious case reviews, 1 April 2007 to 31 March 2008*, Manchester: Office for Standards in Education, Children's Services and Skills.

Ofsted (2009) *Learning lessons from serious case reviews: Year 2*, Manchester: Office for Standards in Education, Children's Services and Skills.

Ofsted (2011) *Good practice by local safeguarding children boards*, Manchester: Office for Standards in Education, Children's Services and Skills.

OPSI (Office of Public Sector Information) (2010) *Safeguarding the future: A review of the youth justice board's governance and operating arrangements*, London: OPSI.

Parton, N. (2006) *Safeguarding childhood: Early intervention and surveillance in a late modern society*, Basingstoke: Palgrave Macmillan.

Preston-Shoot, M. (2009) 'Repeating history? Observations on the development of law and policy for integrated practice', in J. McKimm and K. Phillips (eds) *Leadership and management in integrated services*, Exeter: Learning Matters.

Preston-Shoot, M. (2010) 'Looking after social work practice in its organisational context: neglected and disconcerting questions', in P. Ayre and M. Preston-Shoot (eds) *Children's services at the crossroads: A critical evaluation of contemporary policy for practice*, Lyme Regis: Russell House Publishing.

Rao, V. and Rao, J. (2010) 'Safeguarding children in Madressahs – the experience of Walsall Local Safeguarding Children Board in developing a good practice guide', *Ethnicity and Inequalities in Health and Social Care*, 3(2), pp 32–7.

Rose, W. and Barnes, J. (2008) *Improving safeguarding practice: Study of serious case reviews, 2001–2003*. London: DCSF.

Sidebotham, P., Fox, J., Horwath, J., Powell, C. and Perwez, S. (2008) *Preventing childhood deaths: A study of 'early starter' child death overview panels in England*, London: DCSF.

Social Work Task Force (2009) *Building a safe, confident future: The final report of the Social Work Task Force*, London: DCSF.

Stanley, N. (2010) 'Reasserting the roles of relationships, empathy and training in child protection', *Child Abuse Review*, 19, pp 303–7.

Stanley, N., Miller, P., Richardson Foster, H. and Thomson, G. (2011) 'Children's experiences of domestic violence: developing an integrated response from police and child protection services', *Journal of Interpersonal Violence*, 26(12), pp 2372–91.

Watson, R. (2010) 'Government adviser Andrew Povey questions efficacy of safeguarding boards, YJB and CAFCASS', *Children and Young People Now*, 17 August.

Welbourne, P. (2010) 'Accountability', in L.-A. Long, J. Roche and D. Stringer (eds) *The law and social work: Contemporary issues for practice* (2nd edn), Basingstoke: Palgrave Macmillan.

Welsh Government Guidance (2006) *Safeguarding children: Working together under the Children Act 2004*, Cardiff: Welsh Assembly.

THREE

The child's voice in the child protection system

Jenny Clifton

Eileen Munro wrote in her final report that a child-centred system must recognise that children have rights, including the right to participate in decisions that concern them (Munro, 2011b). Children have made clear that participation is not just about being asked for their views: it is about understanding and being understood, about knowing that their voices have really been heard and how they have been considered. At the heart of this is respect for the child and their experience of their world.

It is a significant step forward for children that the Munro Review frames an improved child protection system in terms of rights and that the Coalition government has supported this approach. While children's right to a voice has been represented in key children's legislation for some time, further action is needed to ensure that they are consistently able to benefit from this right.

The Children's Commissioner has the remit to promote children's rights under the United Nations Convention on the Rights of the Child (UNCRC). This has led to a programme of work gathering children's views and experiences of child protection. The perspectives represented here are drawn from research commissioned by the Children's Commissioner with children still involved in the child protection process (Cossar et al, 2011) and from consultations with children, including those for the Munro Review.

The purpose of this chapter is threefold: to look at what children and young people[1] have said about the child protection system, and in particular whether they feel their voice is heard; to explore how far the Munro Review has reflected these views; and to suggest what it would mean to have the child's voice at the heart of the child protection system. In so doing, this chapter will outline a rights perspective on child protection.

Hearing and acting on the child's voice is only part of what is needed for a child-centred system but it is fundamental. The challenge is to make it a reality for children and young people.

Children's views of the child protection system

Many of the children who met the researchers confirmed the picture we have from earlier studies: they want to see more of their social worker and they want to have greater continuity of relationship with a worker who really gets to know them (Voice, 2005). We wanted to get behind some of these important comments, with the intention of deepening practitioners' understanding and also of informing policy, in the belief that an appreciation of how the child is experiencing the process is vital to effective help.

The children provided considerable insight into the impact of involvement in the child protection process. These were children aged six to 17 for whom the difficulties in the family were not yet fully resolved. While their age had a bearing on the sense they made of the process, an age-appropriate explanation would have improved the understanding of many children (Cossar et al, 2011).

Children's worries

In order to make sense of the child's experience it is necessary to understand their perception of risk. Children may not express their concerns in the terms used by adults. Carolyne Willow (2010) refers to children's emphasis on feelings when talking about protection. Butler and Williamson (1994) have also furthered our understanding of children's perspectives through exploring their worries and anxieties.

Similarly, this research focused on the child's agenda of concerns and therefore asked about children's worries in order to learn about their notion of risk. It was found that these worries were broader than might be anticipated by professionals. There were worries about siblings – about violence experienced at their hands or fear of losing contact through going into care. Others worried about bullying and about violence to their mothers or to themselves from their parents.

The research suggests that professionals need to understand the child's worries and their coping strategies, so they do not underestimate the consequences of these and are better able to make sense of the whole family situation. Conveying this understanding to the child can create a helping alliance and help to relieve the burden of responsibility they feel. The ways in which the children coped with their worries gave an insight into the help they found valuable. Most children were able to talk to trusted friends or family members and could identify a professional who had been helpful. However, some coping strategies were harmful; among these were self-harm and heavy drinking.

Taking responsibility

Children worried about how their behaviour had led to family problems and many felt responsible:

> I don't really think like I'm at risk, it's just my behaviour really, like I don't really feel like I'm in a risky environment or nothing it's just that the things I might say just only to my mum because I might be disrespectful to her, might trigger things off.
>
> (Sol, aged 14, in Cossar et al, 2011: 32)

Children may continue to blame themselves for the problems and the consequences for their family. Others took burdensome responsibility for their parents, aware that there were consequences of their involvement with child protection processes or concerned about their distress: '… and she was crying behind the TV and I comed to her' (Michael, aged 6, in Cossar et al, 2011: 32).

Children's view of professional concerns

Children across the age range were able to find explanations for the social workers' involvement, but these did not always reflect a full understanding and many children disagreed with the professionals' view. For some, this reflected their preparedness to blame themselves and demonstrated loyalty to their family. One young woman had a protection plan on the grounds of emotional abuse and explained how she thought about that:

> [E]motional abuse is where they're like putting you down, calling you fat and ugly and not being there for you. [Mum] doesn't do that though, yeah she puts me down sometimes, she tells me the truth by putting me down if you get me.
>
> (Rachel, aged 16, in Cossar et al, 2011: 44)

Others reflected that social workers had missed important risks. The research indicates the importance of exploring the child's understanding of the family dynamics and of the intervention in their family in an age-appropriate way and ensuring that they are seen alone.

Understanding and participation

Children and young people wanted to make sense of the system in which they were involved. However, most had only a partial grasp. This was related to their age, but a good understanding also resulted from well-supported participation. Children who were not helped by their social worker to gain such understanding were likely to fill in the gaps with information from siblings and others. Few children felt they had been heard in formal meetings, knew how they could be heard, had seen reports or had read their child protection plan.

Children wanted someone they could talk to and did not want to be faced with constant questions:

> It's annoying because like, if I'm having a good day then it's just like, because I know it's going to be the same old questions, is your dad still taking the stuff, and has he ever hit you, it's just like shut up.
>
> (Amy, aged 13, in Cossar et al, 2011: 55)

Such encounters were detrimental to the development of a trusting relationship, as was the experience of words being 'twisted' by professionals. Several children described misrepresentation, exaggeration and words taken out of context. By the same token, valued workers were good listeners: 'She just listens and tries not to get the words muddled around' (Carol, aged 12, in Cossar et al, 2011: 38).

The impact of child protection

Many of the children's responses reflected a mixture of positive and negative views about the services they had received. The negative features of social work involvement included the resultant intrusion, increased tension within the family and having to deal with stigma. Meetings could be 'nerve-wracking' and upsetting. Involvement with child protection could therefore bring additional stress. However, many children had a clear sense of what had helped them and could say what they needed from their social worker.

A good relationship

A good relationship with their worker really made a difference to the nature and extent of their involvement and gave children the sense that 'they were part of making positive changes happen in their families' (Cossar et al, 2011: 12–13):

> He'll research it, come back to me with ideas and if I like the idea we'll put them to the test, like if I was going to get the others together a bit more, work as a function, work as a family, then he'll come up with like take them

> out for a day out, and like I done that this Wednesday, we went out for a day, he took us out.
>
> (Simon, aged 17, in Cossar et al, 2011: 54)

Many gave examples of positive help from their social worker, such as practical assistance, improvements in their family relationships, liaison with schools and talking through their problems. Children stressed the importance of the personal qualities of the social worker and the development of trust: 'you've got to trust her and she's got to trust you; otherwise there's no point' (Louise, aged 15, in Cossar et al, 2011: 54).

A strong link was found between the quality of the relationship with the social worker and the child's ability to have their voice heard. A good relationship helped children manage their worries and could help minimise the negative impact of the child protection process. This research has shown that, without a good understanding of each child's experience, their concerns and the impact of the family dynamics upon them, professionals will not have the child at the centre of their work.

Hearing children's views: some reflections

Children's wishes to have their views taken seriously, both on family problems and on the help they need, have been conveyed to us through a number of consultations on child protection (OCC, 2010, 2011a, 2011b). We learned that it is important to children not just to be heard during the confusing processes of professional decision-making but also to know how their views are taken into account. These consultations have confirmed how much it matters that children's experiences are understood by social workers who become trusted adults and a valued source of support.

The child's voice in the Munro Review

From the first of the three reports produced by Eileen Munro there was evidence of her concern that children's experiences should be 'at the centre of actions, decisions or plans' (Munro, 2010: 19). That report took note of children's wishes to have meaningful relationships with their social workers, the importance of not adding to children's feelings of powerlessness, and their expressed needs from the child protection process.

It is in her second report that Munro addresses the centrality of children's rights under the UNCRC and this is further developed in the final report. She gave the second report the title *The child's journey* in order to emphasise the importance of remaining child-centred and in the final report makes that objective the first principle of an effective child protection system. There is considerable evidence that the views of children and young people influenced the focus of these reports. The detail on social work practice in the second report is highly sensitive to the relationship-based practice children were asking for: 'Above all, it is important to be able to work directly with children and young people to understand their experiences, worries, hopes and dreams' (Munro, 2011a: 37).

The final report's principles for an effective child protection system would meet with the approval of the children we have consulted (Munro, 2011b). For 'everyone in child protection' to pursue child-centred working requires professionals other than social workers to take this seriously. Children's focus on the importance of their family, the emphasis on working *with* children and families, and the value and impact to children of their relationship with their social worker are all reflected there. The principles of providing early help, of variety of response and of making effective impact on children the measure of success all merit further exploration here. The focus below is on the final report.

Child-centred working

A children's definition of what it means for a system to be child-centred was developed by children and adults working together on the Voice Blueprint project (Voice, 2005). Children and young people asked that adults 'see the world as the child sees it', an entreaty relevant to work with children at any age. Their final list included: respect for children as individuals who have something to contribute; working *with* rather than *for* children; putting the needs and interests of children and young people ahead of those of the agencies involved and the adults around them; and respecting young people's competence.

Munro's final report emphasises the importance of communication and relationships, pointing to the significance to children's protection that they are seen and heard. It reflects on the evidence that professionals do not routinely see children and suggests that they may feel inadequately prepared to do so. It is likely that other explanations for the failure of professionals to engage with children are also valid: it can be painful to really listen to children and it takes time (Willow, 2010). The potential for conflicting rights for children and adults in the family, with the latter in a much stronger position, makes insistence on seeing children alone challenging, particularly when there is resistance. This makes direct work skills central to the recruitment and training of social workers and other professionals. It is also necessary to reframe such skills in terms of relationships (Luckock and Lefevre, 2008). Children ask for workers who are concerned enough to truly respect, listen to, engage with and understand them.

Children have requested consistency of worker and asked for time with them alone face-to-face. The Munro reports provide illustrations of good practice and of the impact on the child of having numerous professionals involved. The final report's proposals for reducing prescription, bureaucracy and unnecessarily complicated recording systems, while creating a learning culture and supporting the development of social work expertise, are designed to ensure that more time is available for what social workers want to be doing: helping people directly.

Participation

The report does not expand on the wider meaning of the child's right to participate. However, the section on communication implicitly challenges practitioner attitudes that place limits on listening to children according to their age. As will be discussed later in this chapter, children's rights to a voice and to have that voice heard are not limited by their age, stage of development or ability to communicate in words.

The full implications of a rights-based approach are that children feel they have been heard and that their involvement has made a difference. The child has a right to full consideration of their views and to a judgement which should be transparent. Children and young people have made clear the importance of two-way communication: social workers and others need to offer explanations for decisions made and help children make sense of the system. They do not see the purpose of talking with a social worker as simply to provide information but as part of a meaningful engagement with their lives.

Early help and variety of response

Proposals for early intervention have been criticised for taking a narrow view, with a focus on the early years (Stein, 2011). It is significant therefore that the Munro report uses the phrase 'early help' to apply to the emergence of problems at any age. Given the specific problems faced by older children and young people, it would have been helpful to have a greater focus on the potential response to these.

Many young people face unrecognised abuse and neglect, sexual exploitation, bullying and other violence, long-term mental health problems, and overlapping or multiple disadvantages (Barnes et al, 2011). The consequences for adolescents have been highlighted in a number of recent research reports (Stein et al, 2009; Farmer and Lutman, 2010). Their experience may lead to self-harming and to suicidal or criminal behaviour. In their overview of key research on intervention, Davies and Ward (2011) comment that 'proactive case management may start to diminish for children as young as six'. Recent studies of prevalence demonstrate the extent of unreported abuse (Radford et al, 2011) and our consultations with young people have indicated that they would be unlikely to ask for help with their problems from statutory services.

The child protection system needs to be responsive and relevant to these young people. It is not enough for their problems to be recognised, though that needs to be addressed. There is evidence that the present system is not responsive, and little is known about what approach would work best for young people (Rees et al, 2010). Munro comments on the need for a 'requisite variety' of response and the limitations imposed by procedures. However, it is uncertain how far the use of discretion and professional judgement could address the range of young people's needs. It is doubtful whether an approach which is appropriate for small children can adequately meet the needs of teenagers. There is a need to deliver the kind of service that would enable young people to come forward and ask for help and protection, feeling confident of a response that respects their competence and ability to engage with help. The coordination of services to young people across agencies and accessible early help are both central to this (Rees et al, 2010).

Effective help

Making sure that children benefit from intervention requires feedback from children themselves, not just at times of inspection but as a regular feature of practice. More broadly, young people can be involved directly in inspection processes and projects such as LILAC[2] are enabling them to assess the quality of participation. Young people are also contributing to the selection, training and recruitment of social workers, and there are many good models on which to build.

The report recognises that in order to meet children's needs for workers who are empathic and engage with them, organisations must support their staff, challenge defensive practice and help them build expertise. Good supervision attends to the emotional impact on workers of working with abused children. An 'emotionally intelligent' organisation is vital for the skilled relationship-based practice needed for effective child protection social work (Howe, 2008).

What is a children's rights perspective on child protection?

At the beginning of this chapter, the emphasis of the Munro Review on children's rights as the basis for a child-centred system was welcomed. There are a number of prerequisites if this approach is to be realised and foremost is for professionals to understand the difference a rights approach makes.

Rights and protection

The child's rights under the UNCRC are internationally recognised minimum standards. Children's rights to protection, welfare and participation have been in some measure recognised in specific aspects of UK law.[3] The Convention is a treaty, and as such is binding on all states parties which have signed and ratified it, as the UK did in 1991.

The right to protection is the focus of many of the UNCRC's articles and applies not just to abuse and neglect but also to a wide range of concerns about children's safety and wellbeing.[4] The Convention entitles the child to protection from all forms of violence and encompasses not just children's physical welfare but their emotional wellbeing, healthy development, dignity and worth. A safe environment, the development of their full potential through education and the right to help in recovering from abuse are all part of their protection rights, as is the prevention of harm and the right to equal treatment and protection from discrimination.

The following are fundamental to a rights approach informed by the UNCRC:

- Children have the same rights as adults to respect for their humanity, integrity, privacy and dignity.
- Children's specific rights to protection, to provision to meet their welfare needs and to participation are interrelated.
- A rights analysis considers the balance of power between adults and children and how this can be negotiated in the interests of children.

Participation and protection

Article 12 of the UNCRC states:

> States Parties shall assure to the child who is capable of forming his or her own views the right to express those views freely in all matters affecting the child, the views of the child being given due weight in accordance with the age and maturity of the child.

These rights are reflected in the 1989 Children Act, followed by the 2004 Children Act, which extended the same rights to children in need and in the process of a child protection investigation (Children Act 2004, s 53). The rights apply to all agencies working in a child protection context.

Discussion of children's participation rights often triggers hostility from adults: for some it raises the spectre of children wanting absolute freedom. Mention of rights is therefore often diluted or inseparably linked to 'responsibilities', thus limiting rights to those who can take responsibility for their actions. It may be left out of the discussion of protection altogether on the basis of benevolent and paternalistic or fundamentally discriminatory attitudes to children. The discussions with children represented here have not indicated that children seek absolute freedom: rather, they want adult support and to negotiate ways of being heard. Mary John has challenged false views of the kind of power children seek:

> What is involved in the exercise of children's rights is working towards changing the relationship between adults and children so that, through participation and voicing, each person works towards understanding and respecting each other's realities and points of view. (John, 2003: 269)

Children's participation can improve their protection in the following ways:

- Children will be more likely to be made safe if they can ask for help and will find it hard to have a voice unless they feel safe to express this.
- An understanding of children's own perception and experience of risk enables professionals to take account of their ways of coping and so develop relevant helping strategies.
- Enabling children to have a voice can help to restore integrity and their sense of self-worth: it is essential not to reinforce the powerlessness an abused child has experienced.

- Understanding children's experience of their world provides key information for the assessment of their protection.

A rights-based approach is based on the premise that children merit equal respect on the basis of shared humanity: they are 'full people' in the present, not just future citizens (Alderson, 2000). Taking this perspective leads to a positive view of how children can be seen as active participants in their own lives from a very early age. Priscilla Alderson explores how a rights perspective applies to all children, including the very young. She shows how children's behaviour demonstrates the sense they make of their world and how children engage with and influence this from a very early age, making choices, however constrained these may be (Alderson, 2000). The concept of agency has gained greater currency in recent studies of adolescence and John Coleman emphasises its importance in understanding how young people contribute actively to shaping their own development, linking this to the building of resilience (Coleman, 2011).

Such thinking encourages those who engage with children to start from the assumption that children are competent in understanding, rather than incompetent, and from that perspective to assess, with the child, the kind of participation they wish to have. Consultation and dialogue between adults and children can then be seen as ways of sharing power for the benefit of all on the basis of rights and mutual respect.

Taking rights seriously

The exhortation to respect children's rights will not alone be sufficient to ensure that they are taken seriously. It will be necessary for professionals to challenge their own attitudes and why talk of rights may make them anxious.

Alderson has usefully outlined the kinds of beliefs and strong feelings that lead to adults adopting a position on the merits of consulting children (Alderson, 2011). These can range from a view that children are irresponsible and not competent to a benevolent but paternalistic view that children should not have to worry or feel responsible for decisions. If held inflexibly and without a developmental perspective, these positions can lead to a denial of children's rights (Franklin, 2002; UN, 2009).

For many professionals the main issue is the extent to which children's views are influential or determining, and debates focus on conflicts between a child's views and their best interests. Adults may consider that a child is unlikely to know what is best for them so there is little point in asking for their perspective. Their views may be reported but then sidelined or at worst not gathered at all. Children's best interests, as adults perceive them, and their views may not match but it is important to manage this tension well. The child's perspective on their best interests will provide new insights. Where there are differences, it can be helpful for independent advocates to help the child think through and represent their views. The right to 'due weight' requires a full hearing of the child's voice, transparency about decisions and that children have a good understanding of the reasons when decisions are not as they had hoped.

Willow distinguishes between the *process* and the *outcome* of gaining children's perspectives: the right to be heard is not limited by age or stage, while the weight accorded the child's views is affected by their understanding and age and maturity (Willow, 2010). Recent criminal cases indicate that very young children can bear valid testimony to their experience (Cooper and Wurtzel, 2010; *R v Barker* [2010] EWCA Crim 4). This suggests that issues other than age require careful consideration when giving weight to a child's voice. It is essential to take children's *experiences* seriously as well as their views.

Many children are dependent on adults to help them access their rights. Some do not have a voice because they are considered too young and others because they have complex communication needs. This violates their equality rights under article 2 of the UNCRC. The evidence from our research and consultations is that all children can convey their experiences and what matters to them: the onus is on adults to find ways to hear their voices and to justify overruling their wishes.

What needs to change

The government response to the Munro Review has been generally supportive and has confirmed the importance of the UNCRC as the framework for a proactive child protection system (DfE, 2011). This is encouraging for children. The initial government response did not take up the recommendations to research the impact of health service reorganisation and hesitated to establish a duty for the provision of early help. The question remains as to whether the child protection system can respond effectively to the needs of young people without such a duty, particularly in the context of cuts to local services and recently recognised risks for which the current arrangements have proved inadequate.

It is suggested that for children's voices to be at the heart of the child protection process and to be taken into account, the following three steps are prerequisites:

1. Taking rights seriously: a task for the whole system

Children have rights to protection, to provision and to participation. It is important to overcome reluctance to use this terminology and to address the fundamental right of all children to be safe and to be emotionally as well as physically nourished. Helping children to access these rights is an obligation on all those with a brief to protect children and reflects the traditional concerns of social work.

The rights perspective leads to a broad concept of protection and embraces the needs of all: young people in the criminal justice system; those who are sexually exploited; those with mental health problems; young asylum seekers. It requires us to reframe risky, troublesome behaviour as evidence of need.

2. Meeting the protection needs of older children and young people

There is a clear need for a child protection system that is relevant, responsive and accessible to older children and young people, and one which they trust. This would require a proactive approach that enables vulnerable young people to ask for help and extends support to them. Such a service would ensure that all children and young people are aware of their right to protection and can be confident of a positive response.

3. Making relationships which last

The structure of the service needs to be designed to maximise the opportunity for children to have continuity of relationships with those helping them. This in itself is an agenda for child protection and broader children's services. It connects with plans for the retention of social workers in practice roles, with the valuing of the social work role, the recruitment of workers who want to sustain their involvement with children, the development of new team models and with the training agenda.

At the conclusion of the research on their views, children and young people sent their messages for change to the Children's Commissioner (Cossar et al, 2011: 83–85). Among the many telling contributions, these represent clearly the themes of this chapter:

> Listen to what children have to say and work with them.
>
> Don't be overly negative. Focus on the good bits as well as the not so good.
>
> Be lenient with children, let them do things, but be there for them and let them know you're there.

Acknowledgement

I would like to thank Marian Brandon and Jeanette Cossar for their helpful comments on an earlier draft of this chapter.

Notes

[1] To avoid repetition, the term 'child' includes 'young person'.

[2] A project run by A National Voice entitled 'Leading Improvements for Looked After Children' (www.lilacanv.org).

[2] See UK government report on UNCRC incorporation 2010. The Coalition government's commitment to the UNCRC has been

clearly stated. However, the UN committee outlined continuing concerns about the realisation of children's rights in its 2008 report.

[3] Articles 6, 16, 17, 19, 24, 28, 32, 34, 35, 37 and 39 are all relevant to the rights to protection.

References

Alderson, P. (2000) *Young children's rights*, London: Save the Children, Jessica Kingsley.

Barnes, M., Green, R. and Ross, A. (2011) *Understanding vulnerable young people: Analysis from the longitudial study of young people in England*, NatCen, DfE Research Report DFE-RR118, London: DfE.

Butler, I. and Williamson, H. (1994) *Children speak: Children, trauma and social work*, Essex: NSPCC, Longman.

Coleman, J. (2011) *The nature of adolescence*, London: Routledge.

Cooper, P. and Wurtzel, D. (2010) 'A good day for child witnesses' (*R v Barker*; EWCA Crim 4), *Criminal Law and Justice Weekly*, 13 February.

Cossar, J., Brandon, M. and Jordan, P. (2011) *Don't make assumptions: Children's and young people's views of the child protection system and messages for change,* London: OCC.

Davies, C. and Ward, H. (2011) *Safeguarding children across services: Messages from research*, London: Jessica Kingsley. Available at: www.education.gov.uk/publications/RSG/AllRsgPublications/Page4/DFE-RBX-10-09

DfE (Department for Education) (2011) *A child-centred system: The government's response to the Munro Review of Child Protection*, London: DfE. Available at: www.education.gov.uk/publications.

Farmer, E. and Lutman, E. (2010) *Case management and outcomes for neglected children returned to their parents: A five-year follow up study*, DCSF-RB214, London: Department for Children, Schools and Families (DCSF).

Franklin, B. (ed) (2002) *The new handbook of children's rights,* London: Routledge.

Howe, D. (2008) *The emotionally intelligent social worker*, Basingstoke: Palgrave Macmillan.

John, M. (2003) *Children's rights and power: Charging up for a new century*, London: Jessica Kingsley.

Luckock, B. and Lefevre, M. (eds) (2008) *Direct work: Social work with children and young people in care*, London: BAAF.

Munro, E. (2010) *The Munro Review of Child Protection: Part 1: A systems analysis*, London: The Stationery Office, p 21.

Munro, E. (2011a) *The Munro Review of Child Protection: Interim report: The child's journey*, London: The Stationery Office. Available at: www.education.gov.uk/publications.

Munro, E. (2011b) *The Munro Review of Child Protection: Final report: A child-centred system*, London: The Stationery Office. Available at: www.education.gov.uk/publications.

OCC (Office of the Children's Commissioner) (2010) 'Submission to the Munro Review of Child Protection', September, London.

OCC (2011a) *Do more than listen: Act* [a report for the Family Justice Council undertaken for the Family Justice Review], London. Available at: www.childrenscommissioner.gov.uk.

OCC (2011b) 'Response to the interim report of the Family Justice Review'. Available at: www.childrenscommissioner.gov.uk.

Radford, L., Corral, S., Bradley, C., Fisher, H., Bassett, C., Howat, N. and Collishaw, S. (2011) *Child abuse and neglect in the UK today*, London: NSPCC.

Rees, G., Gorin, S., Jobe, A., Stein, M., Medforth, R. and Goswami, H. (2010) *Safeguarding young people: Responding to young people aged 11 to 17 who are maltreated*, London: Children's Society.

Stein, M., Rees, G., Hicks, L. and Gorin, S. (2009) *Neglected adolescents: Literature review*, DCSF-RBX-09-04, London: DCSF.

Stein, M. (2011) 'The fixation on early years intervention is naïve'. Available at: www.guardian.co.uk/society/joepublic/2011/jan/11/fixation-early-years-intervention-flawed (accessed 18 September 2011).

UN (United Nations) (2009) Committee on the Rights of the Child, fifty-first session, Geneva. Available at: http://www2.ohchr.org/english/bodies/crc/comments (accessed 18 September 2011).

Voice (2005) *Start with the child, stay with the child: A blueprint for a child centred approach to children and young people in public care*, London: Voice (formerly Voice for the Child in Care).

Willow, C. (2010) *Children's right to be heard and effective child protection*, Sweden: Save the Children.

FOUR

Parental mental health, risk and child protection: what does Munro mean to child protection and adult mental health?

Andrew Coombe

Introduction

Parents with mental health problems can present particular difficulties for health and social care services concerned with child health, child protection and adult mental health. Many children living with parents with mental illness suffer no harm and young carers may even find benefits in the relationship. However, potential harm to children may be immediate and life-threatening, particularly if the child features in the parent's delusional or suicidal ideas. This chapter explores what we know about children who suffer a negative developmental impact from mentally ill parents and is supported by data from studies of serious case reviews (SCRs) undertaken across England and Wales in recent years (Coombe, 2010). It demonstrates the importance of close collaboration between adult mental health practitioners and those working in the child protection system. The conclusion is stark. What levers do the changes currently espoused by the Munro Review (Munro, 2011) and the government response (DfE, 2011) bring to such a liaison? And what should policymakers and strategic managers expect of practitioners in primary and secondary health services who interface with the child protection system around accountability and management of risk?

This chapter concludes that, when it comes to professional decision-making and assessment of risk, professionals continue to focus on the individual who is the remit of their services rather than the family. In this case, how can Munro have the impact needed on multi-agency working and how will current changes to health commissioning and service delivery help the child's journey? Conflicts of interest already occur between child-focused and adult-focused services as a result of working to different agendas, legislation and guidance and it is not clear whether the broad-brush changes put forward by Munro will have the required impact.

In the White Paper *Equity and excellence: Liberating the NHS* (DH, 2010), there are clear references to the roles and responsibilities of GP consortia (subsequently renamed clinical commissioning groups) and health and wellbeing boards in safeguarding. Since then, consultation documents and papers related to NHS reforms have continued to reinforce the statutory requirements relating to child protection, culminating in the government response to the NHS future forums report:

> The NHS and other health organisations have a critical role in preventing and identifying abuse, neglect and exploitation of vulnerable adults and children, and we will ensure that the leaders of all health organisations recognise and fulfil their safeguarding responsibilities. (DH, 2011a)

Despite this reassurance, the future of child protection is unclear in the NHS and Munro does not shed light on the detail. Nationally there are already concerns about the scale and pace of the NHS reforms and a real fear that this will result in a loss of focus on safeguarding and a dilution of specialist practitioners such as designated professionals. Munro has reinforced the importance of the role of senior paediatrician and senior nurse to take the professional lead and also expressed concern about the impact of NHS reform on child safeguarding.

What we already know: SCRs and parental mental health

A number of national reports and reviews give us information about the frequency that mental health problems have been identified in a parent/parents. In the second to last biennial review of SCRs (Brandon et al, 2009), a study of 189 reviews from 2005 to 2007, parental mental health problems were identified in 32 cases. Of the more detailed analysis of 40 cases in the same study, current or past mental health problems in either parent were identified in 25 cases (63%). In a review of 60 SCRs completed by the London Safeguarding Children Board, 60% of families had a parent with mental health problems that affected childcare (London SCB, 2010).

The National Confidential Inquiry into Suicides and Homicides reviewed 254 homicide convictions between 1997 and 2004 in England and Wales where children were killed by their biological parent or step-parent. Of these, 37% (94 out of 254) had a mental disorder, including 15% with depressive illness or bipolar affective disorder, 11% with personality disorder, 8% with schizophrenia or other delusional disorders, and 5% with substance or alcohol dependence (NPSA, 2009).

Between April 2007 and March 2008, Ofsted evaluated 50 SCRs and found that mental illness featured in 14 and was not always appropriately considered as part of the risk assessment to children. The level of involvement of mental health NHS trusts and other specialist services varied. In some cases, they had been very involved in assessments and treatment programmes, and were key contributors to the SCR. In others, they were notable by their absence, either because they had not been identified as key partners or because of an unwillingness to get involved (Ofsted, 2008).

In an unpublished report, one Local Safeguarding Children Board in 2009 identified adult mental health issues in 21 cases (88%). Sixteen mothers and four fathers were recorded as having mental health issues, with depression the most frequently recorded diagnosis. The data above on parental mental health and SCRs or homicides are summarised in Table 1.

Table 1: Percentage of parental mental illness identified in studies and reports

Author	Type of case reviewed	Number of cases	% where parental mental health problems were identified
LSCB (2009, unpublished)	SCR	24	88
Brandon et al (2009)	SCR	40	63
London SCB (2010)	SCR	60	60
Brandon et al (2008)	SCR	47	55
NCISH (2006)	Homicide	254	37
NCI (unpublished)	Filicide	245	35
Falkov (1996)	SCR	100	32
Ofsted (2008)[1]	SCR	50	28

[1] The Ofsted report included children with mental health problems as well as parents

Recent well-publicised events in the press such as the deaths of Peter Connelly ('Baby P') and Khyra Ishaq have increased public awareness, and in both cases mental health problems in the parent/carer were suggested. In a newspaper article on Baby P's mother, Tracey Connelly, *The Sun* reported that friends had 'noticed her interest in Peter was waning, while a health visitor rejected her claims to be suffering from post-natal depression' (Peake and France, 2009). *The Daily Record*'s (2010) article on Connelly's boyfriend, Steven Barker – also convicted of Peter Connelly's murder – reported that he suffered from depression and had been the victim of sexual abuse as a child. In the case of Khyra Ishaq, *The Daily Telegraph* reported that Khyra's mother, Angela Gordon, had suffered from major depression and her boyfriend, also convicted of manslaughter and child cruelty, was a schizophrenic (Gammell and Cockroft, 2010).

Any child death is tragic, particularly when it is the result of abuse or neglect. Deaths that occur at the hands of parents are relatively rare. For example, in 2009/10 there were 52 homicide victims under the age of 16; of these, 69% were killed by their parents – 36 offences (Smith et al, 2011). To put this in context, the population of children under the age of 16 was just over 11.6 million at the time (ONS estimates, mid-2010). However, given a particular set of political conditions, these tragic and highly publicised incidents can produce circumstances that confront policymakers with a type of 'forced choice'.

As Fox writes in his chapter on SCRs (see this volume, Chapter 7) the findings of Professor Munro on SCRs indicate that this approach to learning lessons where children have been harmed may not be particularly effective. Indeed, there have been critiques of the system of inquiry for some time. Warner (2006) argues that major inquiries are fundamentally flawed because their function and structure make 'hindsight bias' inevitable; as a result, a poor outcome is always going to be associated with poor decision-making. The net impact of this on professionals is to raise anxiety and promote defensive practice for fear of becoming the next focus of an SCR following a child death. Brandon et al (2009) found that the process of SCRs had an overwhelmingly negative impact on the majority of practitioners interviewed, with articulated feelings of failure, guilt, fear and anxiety, and words like 'threatening', 'traumatic', 'devastating' and 'stressful' used on many occasions (Warner, 2006: 103). Practitioners reported a lack of support and supervision and a feeling of isolation throughout the process.

In the decade since the development of the National Patient Safety Agency, the NHS has adopted a root cause analysis methodology process developed from other safety-conscious fields such as the aviation industry. Root cause analysis (RCA) is a component of the broader field of total quality management, which has arisen from the world of business management. It has been defined as a structured investigation that aims to identify the true cause of a problem and the actions necessary to eliminate it, and utilises a number of tools for this approach including the 'five whys', brainstorming processes and fishbone diagrams (see also www.nrls.npsa.nhs.uk). This process is used very effectively in some areas of patient safety such as healthcare-acquired infections, but is more difficult to apply in complex multi-agency circumstances. The process is unlikely to uncover some previously unknown fundamental (root) cause, but rather point to areas of interagency working that require improvement.

The government response to Munro (DfE, 2011) states that 'current arrangements for SCRs reinforce a prescriptive approach towards practice' with too much emphasis on a blame culture. It agrees with Munro that systems review methodology should be used by local safeguarding children boards (LSCBs) when SCRs are undertaken. Broadly, this is to be welcomed but the emphasis on these investigations, whatever methodology is used, is sometimes unhelpful. There is also a danger that we focus too intently on SCRs and assume that the problems found are representative of the system. In Munro's words: 'Such tragic cases are not representative of the majority of professional work and therefore, while remaining important, it is unwise to premise the majority of organisational development on them.'

Why it is important that we gain a better understanding of the impact of parental mental health on children

The majority of parents with a history of mental ill health present no risk to their children (Glaser et al, 2004; DCSF, 2010). Tunnard (2004) reports that the quality of parent–child interactions occurs across very wide spectrums, from impressive parenting to serious child injury or death. While some children grow up apparently unscathed, others exhibit emotional and behavioural disorders as a result of these childhood experiences (Wier and Douglas, 1999; DH, 2000), and it is important therefore that any changes to service delivery arising out of the Munro Review and the government response take heed of the current organisational limitations between adult and children's services. At its most extreme, children with parents who are mentally ill may be abused and suffer significant harm through physical, sexual, emotional or psychological abuse, or be exposed to significant levels of neglect (Kaplan, 1999; DH, 2000; DCSF, 2010). The children of delusional parents are at risk of parental coercion, isolation and physical danger, which results in poor social functioning, anxiety and lack of a sense of self, both in the short term and long term (Ahern, 2003). This is therefore of concern for those of us working with highly vulnerable children, young people and families.

Higher rates of psychiatric morbidity and psychosocial problems have been found among caregivers of abused children compared to control groups. The behavioural problems of abused children are not only strongly affected by their experience of being abused but are also related to mental health problems and psychosocial risk factors found in their mothers (Takei et al, 2006). Overall, children with mothers who have mental ill health are five times more likely to have mental health problems themselves (DCSF, 2010).

Protective factors include the child's age, gender and developmental stage, the availability of other caring relationships, the parents' level of functioning, and intrinsic factors within the child themselves such as temperament, individual personality and degree of resilience (Bird, 1999; Stanley et al, 2003; DCSF, 2010). Environmental risk factors may also include the levels of stress or life events in the household, the availability of wider family or social support, social/educational status of the parents, the size of the family, and whether the child has been placed in care (Kaplan, 1999).

Just as there is a range of symptoms and severity of illness, so there is a range of potential impacts on families (DCSF, 2010). Undetected and poorly managed maternal depression and associated child adjustment problems are common health problems and impose significant burdens on society (Elgar, 2004). Children may not receive sufficient care and stimulation to fully develop their potential, and may not develop sufficient skills through observing their own parents to be able – in due course – to parent their own children effectively. They may feel unable to engage fully in social relationships and be vulnerable to bullying and social isolation as a result, particularly in schools (Wier and Douglas, 1999). Falkov (1996, cited in Stanley, 2003: 9) suggests that children can experience impaired development in a number of areas, including 'cognitive development, language, attention and concentration span, educational achievement and social, emotional and behavioural development'.

In the children of depressed mothers, insecure attachment, developmental delay, educational and social difficulties, and the development of specific psychopathological syndromes have all been identified (Bird, 1999). Depression can result in the individual experiencing feelings of worthlessness and lack of hope, which may lead to everyday activities being left undone. As a result, parents may neglect their own and their children's physical and emotional needs (DCSF, 2010).

In certain conditions (such as some personality disorders) there may be parental over-involvement, which may take the form of harsh criticism or discipline. Marked personality disorders can have the most negative impact on children, particularly where repeated episodes of attempted suicide, often witnessed by children, may not necessarily reflect severe mental illness but instead be a symptom of failing coping skills, including serious difficulties in parenting (Glaser et al, 2004).

In many cases, children become 'young carers'. Of the 175,000 young carers identified in the 2001 census, 29% – or just over 50,000 – are estimated to care for a family member with mental health problems (Dearden and Becker, 2004, cited in SCIE, 2009: 8).

A child's safety will be more at risk in families where mental health problems have been psychotic in nature and have coexisted with other mental health difficulties or issues arising from social deprivation. In extreme situations, a child may be killed or seriously harmed, with infants being particularly vulnerable (Kaplan, 1999). In a review of filicides[1] in 2009, Flynn (2008) found that the most at risk age group for homicide is 12 months or under. From a sample of 254 filicides, data from the National Confidential Inquiry (unpublished) found that over a third of parents were mentally ill at the time of the offence (NPSA, 2009).

Parents who have repeatedly self-harmed, who have threatening delusions and hallucinations, and those who include their children in their symptoms may pose a particular risk to children (DCSF, 2010). Parker supports this view:

> Perhaps of most concern are those parents who have a chronic psychotic disorder and who involve their children in their delusions. Either the children are part of their delusional system or they expect the children to behave in a way which is compatible with the delusion. (Parker, 1999: 26)

In May 2009, the National Patient Safety Agency (NPSA) identified that very serious risks may arise if a parent's illness incorporates delusional beliefs about the child, as well as the potential for the parent to harm the child as part of a suicide plan, and required mental health organisations to respond to a number of actions. The rationale for many of the actions was as a result of previous failings, including where:

- assessment of risks to children was not triggered because there was no recognition that contact with children had been resumed;
- assessment of risks to children was inadequate owing to the service user's assurance that they were symptom-free and/or compliant with treatment;
- organisations had inappropriately delegated key decision-making for patients known to have delusional beliefs about their children (for example, decisions on granting home leave were made by junior medical staff).

The limitations of single agency approaches

Parenting capacity is one of three domains for assessment in Department of Health guidance *Framework for the assessment of children in need and their families* (DH, 2000), which identifies parental mental health problems as a factor which can adversely affect a parent's ability to respond to the needs of the child. It is often the adult psychiatrist who is asked to give an opinion about the parenting capacity. In their pilot study, Stanley and Penhale identified examples where social workers had asked adult psychiatrists to assess mothers' parenting capacity. They concluded that the high status given to medical practitioners may give rise to confusion about the appropriate contribution of psychiatric expertise to the assessment of capacity: 'the psychiatric assessment can inform the assessment of parenting but should not be a substitute for it' (cited in Stanley et al, 2003: 117). Measuring parenting capacity relies on the understanding and ability of professionals to make judgements about parenting and children's needs based on criteria such as the nature of parent–child relationships, parental characteristics and parents' abilities to prioritise children's needs (Aldridge, 2006). Reder and Duncan (1997) argue strongly that general psychiatrists' skills are best confined to an appraisal of the parents' mental state and prognosis. Subsequent guidance issued by the Royal College of Psychiatrists in 2004 is clear that the role of the adult psychiatrist is to provide an assessment of the parent's diagnosis, prognosis and functioning rather than a specific assessment of parenting capacity (Glaser et al, 2004).

The children of parents with severe mental health problems are very likely to be classified as 'children in need' in the scope of the 1989 Children Act, although this may vary according to local authority eligibility criteria for services. This does not mean that all parents with mental health problems are poor parents or that children cannot cope with parents who are unstable or unpredictable; however, it should ensure that the child's care and development is kept under review independently of the needs of the parents (Bernard and Douglas, 1999). However, the Children Act leaves us in no doubt that the needs of the children are paramount in all Children Act court proceedings where a conflict of interest arises between the needs of the parent and the child (Beck-Sander, 1999).

One of the factors reported by parents with mental health problems is the adversarial nature of child protection processes. The scenario of child protection procedures and conferences can place a huge stress and pressure on parents, who may already be vulnerable as a result of their mental health problems. For many people, not only those with mental health problems, the suggestion of involving social services 'evokes the spectre of their children being removed, with the implied loss of responsibility and control' (Parker, 1999: 23). If the parent supposes that the professionals involved are blaming and punishing them for their ill health, their self-esteem may fall, their sense of guilt may increase and their ability to provide parental care will reduce. The resulting stress can be manifested in aggression, demoralisation or exacerbation of their mental health problem (Kaplan, 1999). Stanley et al (2003) found that mothers' negative experiences of childcare services could deter them from accessing support for their mental health problems early, as they judged that this could jeopardise their continuing care of their children. Professionals are then deprived of the opportunity to assess families in a situation where parental mental health needs are mild or deteriorating rather than acute. Similarly, Aldridge (2006) argues that what prevents adults with mental health problems from seeking parenting support is their fear of child protection procedures and professional interventions that only serve to further undermine parenting roles. This is illustrated by extracts from SCRs reported by Kingston SCB in 2008:

> The focus of attention was on the mother's mental health problems (which were complex), leading to assumptions that the difficulties with the children were due to her poor parenting.... The mother felt wholly criticised for poor parenting with no positive encouragement, leading her into further mental health problems due to sense of inadequacy and loss of identity.

and from Birmingham SCB, also in 2008:

> ... the approach that social care took in their assessment left the mother thinking that the only option was for the child to come into care. This discouraged her from pursuing this and getting additional help because of her experience when she was admitted to hospital.

In her final report, Munro also recognises the risks of overestimating the danger to the child and that people react strongly when they see families being broken up and perceive that professionals are getting too powerful. Striking a balance between the needs of the parent and the needs of the child is not easy – there may well be a conflict of interest between professionals. There are powerful tensions between the rights of children and the needs of parents, who themselves are under stress due to their mental ill health (Kaplan, 1999; Parker, 1999; Wier and Douglas, 1999; Darlington et al, 2004; Johnson, 2009). Effective collaboration between child protection and mental health services is difficult to achieve. Potential organisational barriers include a lack of agency-level structures and policies, inadequate resources, poor communication, unrealistic expectations and differences in protocols or policies (Darlington et al, 2005). The mental illness of a parent can also introduce difficult behaviours that present a range of challenges to child protection professionals, including poor insight and an inability to differentiate between their own needs and those of their children. Other challenges include the episodic and/or unpredictable nature of the illness and the lack of any continuity if people with mental illness move accommodation on a frequent basis (Darlington et al, 2004).

A few decades ago, people with mental health problems were subjected to compulsory sterilisation programmes through the entrenched cultural belief that people diagnosed as mentally ill were unable to parent:

> Underlying all the arguments was the presumption that it is socially desirable to prevent the creation of new human beings who might be mentally ill or feeble-minded. They might diminish the gene pool, they might contribute to crime and prostitution, and they might be expensive. (Sayce, 1999: 29)

Within many health services, there remains an assumption of a lack of parenting capacity in people with significant mental health problems. Offers of family interventions such as family therapy tend to be restricted to situations where the child is the identified patient (Parker, 1999). In the context of mothers with mental health needs, research has tended to focus on adverse outcomes. Positive outcomes and successes for children and parents with mental health problems are rarely noted (Stanley et al, 2003). Few adult psychiatry departments have close working relationships with child and family services (Bird, 1999). In 1996, Falkov concluded:

> … child care professionals lacked an understanding of parental mental health needs and that those working in adult services placed little emphasis on child protection and the child's care and welfare. (Falkov, 1996, cited in Stanley, 2003: 39)

For childcare staff, the weight of professional anxiety caused by the potential risks and the impact of negative labelling may cause them to act prematurely in removing children from the care of their parents (Bernard and Douglas, 1999). For mental health staff, particularly psychiatrists, it is usually the adult who is their prime concern and hence they may feel that their primary responsibility lies towards the patient and what they consider to be in their best interests. Adult psychiatry tends to have an individual focus and pays considerable attention to diagnostic precision (Reder and Duncan, 1997). Psychiatrists may feel that overriding the wishes of their patient (the parent) may potentially harm future therapeutic relationships (Parker, 1999), and collaboration with social services can be seen as a threat to the therapeutic alliance (Glaser et al, 2004): 'it is a common experience that adult psychiatrists and mental health workers often do not know whether or not their patients have any children' (Göpfert et al, 1996, cited in Aldridge, 2006).

Each agency has different thresholds for intervention and different definitions of significant harm. Variations exist in the eligibility criteria for access to family support through social care and in the referral criteria for specialist psychiatric care (Tye and Precey, 1999). The government policy responses to risks posed by adults with mental health and to children are not linked: for example, there are supervision registers for adults and child protection plans. They are maintained by different agencies with different decision-making processes required for names to be added to them. Child protection and mental health staff work in these separate worlds, supported by parallel but uncoordinated guidance and legislation, and may fail to see the full picture when families have complex needs. If communication between these groups of professionals is poor, or they lack basic knowledge of each other's systems, then risks to both children and their parents inevitably increase (Bernard and Douglas, 1999). While comparing services across Europe for supporting families with a mentally ill parent, Hetherington and Baistow found:

> It was common for mental health professionals to feel unsure of themselves in working with children, while child welfare professionals felt that they lacked knowledge of mental illness. However, the level of understanding of mental illness held in child welfare teams varied considerably. (Hetherington and Baistow, 2001: 357)

The Munro Review offers an opportunity to improve the links between adult mental health services and the child protection system. Munro is clear that the revised inspection framework should examine the effectiveness of the contributions of all local services, including health, education, police, probation and the justice system, to the protection of children. Surely this also means adult mental health services. She also reinforces the need to analyse data relevant to safeguarding from all local agencies.

Improved multi-agency working is a recurrent theme in mental health recommendations in SCRs (Coombe, 2010) and includes setting up joint working groups, improving joint working, developing joint assessments and improving liaison and communication. This problem is not a recent one, and it would be foolish to assume that services worked more effectively together in the past, but the specialisation of services in the past two decades has contributed to the demarcation and lack of communication between professionals (Wier and Douglas, 1999).

Child abuse and neglect rarely occur independently of other stresses and circumstances and cannot be effectively responded to in isolation. The tendency towards 'silo practice' found by Brandon et al (2009), where professionals preferred to work in the comfort zone of their own specialism, underlines the importance of joint child protection working, frequently mentioned in recommendations from the 2007–10 SCR executive summaries. The tendency of these recommendations is to stipulate multi-agency training as a mechanism for this; however, there are risks if training is not effectively targeted and continues to be accessed on a 'first come, first served basis'.

Child health services and mental health services operate in their own worlds of ethical issues and unique languages. The interpretation of such concepts as confidentiality, civil liberties and the 'paramountcy principle' is specific to each organisation (Tye and Precey, 1999). Common ways of seeing the world must be found by each agency in order to work together. In their discussions on systems theory, Japp and Kusche (2008) argue that modern society is divided into subsystems, with no system being more important than another and no particular hierarchy existing between them. This is in contrast to the 'early modern era', where society was differentiated according to social class, primarily formed by birthrights and characterised by a religious and moral authority. In that historical context, it was almost certain that the medical practitioners' authority would reign supreme and would not be doubted by other professionals.

Significant changes occurred in social care through the final decades of the 20th century, with a shift from generic to specialist social work and the development of separate care groups such as older people, physical disability, learning disability, mental health, and children and families. This enabled those care groups to receive dedicated attention and specialist skills from practitioners, but created boundaries, overlaps, service gaps and transition issues. There is now evidence of fragmentation, with separate services on separate sites, accessed through different mechanisms and managed by different agencies (Wier and Douglas, 1999). The move from generic to specialist practice happened quickly and 'unwritten and unspoken demarcation and barriers quickly became apparent' (Diggins, 1999: 138). Social workers also reported feeling 'quickly deskilled in working with user groups outside their own specialism' (Diggins, 1999: 139).

Over the corresponding period in mental health services, the shift was from care provided in large Victorian asylums to care in the community, with an expectation that the family would be expected to assume more responsibility for its members who suffered from mental health problems (Cox, 1999). Along with the policy shift towards community care, improvements in medication have enabled patients to manage their illnesses better (Hetherington and Baistow, 2001). The net result is that parents have come to spend more time with their families, including dependent children (Tunnard, 2004). In mental health services, there has also been a move towards specialised services with the separation into specialist areas such as 'acute', 'community', 'forensic mental health', 'early intervention services', as well as the separation between 'primary' (GP-led) and 'secondary' (specialist-led), previously mentioned. This creates difficulties for staff in terms of a lack of knowledge and experience of their colleagues' specialism and the potential for poor communication and transfer of information between these services (for example, basic information such as whether or not the patient has any children).

The White Paper *Equity and excellence: Liberating the NHS* (DH, 2010) set out a number of key principles for reform: shared decision-making, access to information, choice of provider and personalised care. The paper is strong on accountability and choice but weak on protecting vulnerable groups in society: those who cannot make decisions for themselves. GP commissioning and health and wellbeing board responsibility in relation to safeguarding is not entirely clear. Some PCTs have already transferred their responsibility for designated staff to local authorities, or are in the throes of doing so, and although the NHS reforms are geared towards local decision-making – *'no decision about me, without me'* – this approach may serve to weaken the progress that has been made nationally in protecting children.

The government response to Munro (DfE, 2011) is light on the role of mental health services in the child protection system but does make reference to the importance of cluster PCT chief executives retaining a local lead in multi-agency accountability for the safety and welfare of children. On 31 October 2011 the government published *Safeguarding children in the reformed NHS: a co-produced work programme between the Department of Health, Department for Education, and national and local stakeholders* (DH, 2011b) to review how the health reforms will prioritise safeguarding. Designated roles and named professionals are likely to remain, and as clinical commissioning groups become more clearly defined, it is envisaged that governance and accountability arrangements between LSCBs and new health and wellbeing boards will be outlined at local level. However, without drawing on the lessons learned from SCRs to date, and looking at the evidence base in relation to the impact of parental mental health on children, there is a danger that local health reforms will 'fragment leadership and professional responsibility locally for child protection and safeguarding' (DfE, 2011):

> There remains a critical role for a senior paediatrician and a senior nurse to take a strategic, professional lead on all aspects of the health service contribution to safeguarding children within the local area. This role includes the provision of expert advice on commissioning across

> the whole health economy and to the LSCB, and the provision of overall leadership and direction. (Munro, 2011)

Conclusion

This chapter concludes that organisations need to guard against seeing SCRs as the only tool to understand themes in child deaths and injuries, given that the vast majority of professionals in child and mental health services have not experienced that process. It is clear that, for them, it is difficult to apply learning to their practice. Professionals will often use their own professional judgement, skills and experience and subjective strategies such as intuition to make complex decisions in autonomous situations, rather than adopt a methodical adherence to policy. In any case, single agency protocols and policies are unlikely to take into account the multiple complex and interacting risk factors that are evident in many of these tragic cases. We are heavily reliant on practitioners 'in the field' to respond effectively to child protection concerns.

There are opportunities through the Munro reforms for organisations and LSCBs to consider the evidence drawn out of SCRs more closely and work towards improving preventative activities such as regular local learning opportunities to consider risks posed by already well-known complex and risky families. Screening and assessment should be more sophisticated – it is not enough to identify parental mental health as a risk factor without a fuller understanding of the diagnosis, prognosis and impact on the parents' functioning. This can only be achieved if both adult mental health and child protection services have a better awareness of, and respect for, each other's statutory requirements, operational policies and work pressures. The development of local practice development groups based on real experiences and case studies can be a useful tool to identify common blocks in practice and promote successful strategies to overcome difficulties and conflicts.

Moreover, with the strengthening of LSCBs as multi-agency scrutiny bodies, there is a possibility to use the Munro reforms to reiterate the importance of multi-agency training for frontline staff. This includes primary and secondary health practitioners as well as those working in the child protection system. Professionals need to accept that it is unlikely that a full understanding of each other's perspectives will be always reached. Rather, it is necessary to acknowledge differences due to different professional viewpoints, different systems and processes and, sometimes, conflicting guidance and legislation. Only then can teams in different services start to work more effectively together to consider the risks to the families with whom they are involved.

It is unlikely that the Munro Review and the government's response will have an extensive impact on mental health services. Changes to the SCR process, the development of performance indicators and a review of inspection to include all agencies are important steps but will not necessarily change practice on the ground. In the longer term, it will be the responsibility of the health commissioners to translate Munro's recommendations into practice on the frontline. However, with the massive scale and rapid pace of NHS reforms, there is a risk that health might 'drop the ball'. The future of safeguarding in the NHS is less than clear and, so far, clinical commissioning groups have shown little appetite to take on these statutory functions.

Note

[1] The term filicide denotes a form of homicide in which a parent kills his or her own child.

References

Ahern, K. (2003) 'At-risk children: a demographic analysis of the children attending mental health community clinics', *International Journal of Mental Health Nursing*, 12, pp 223–8.

Aldridge, J. (2006) 'The experiences of children living with and caring for parents with mental illness', *Child Abuse Review*, 15, pp 79–88.

Beck-Sander, A. (1999) 'Working with parents with mental health problems: management of the many risks', in A. Wier and A. Douglas (eds) *Child protection and mental health: Conflict of interest?*, Oxford: Butterworth Heinemann, pp 69–77.

Bernard, J. and Douglas, A. (1999) 'The size of the task facing professional agencies', in A. Wier and A. Douglas (eds) *Child protection and mental health: Conflict of interest?*, Oxford: Butterworth Heinemann, pp 109–36.

Bird, A. (1999) 'Families coping with mental health problems: the role and perspective of the general adult psychiatrist', in A. Wier and A. Douglas (eds) *Child protection and mental health: Conflict of interest?*, Oxford: Butterworth Heinemann, pp 17–22.

Brandon, M., Belderson, P., Warren, C., Howe D., Gardner, R., Dodsworth, J. and Black, J. (2008) *Analysing child deaths and serious injury through abuse and neglect: What can we learn? A biennial analysis of serious case reviews 2003–2005*, London: DCSF.

Brandon, M., Bailey, S., Belderson, P., Gardner, R., Sidebotham, P., Dodsworth, J., Warren, C. and Black, J. (2009) *Understanding serious case reviews and their impact: A biennial analysis of serious case reviews 2005–2007*, London: The Stationery Office.

Coombe, A. (2010) *Parental mental health, risk and child protection*, dissertation (unpublished), Centre for Health Services Studies, University of Kent.

Cox, J.L. (1999) 'Postnatal depression in the context of changing patterns of childcare: the implications for primary prevention', in A. Wier and A. Douglas (eds) *Child protection and mental health: Conflict of interest?*, Oxford: Butterworth Heinemann, pp 63–77.

Darlington, Y., Feeney, J.A. and Rixon, K. (2004) 'Complexity, conflict and uncertainty: issues in collaboration between child protection and mental health services', *Children and Youth Services Review*, 26, pp 1175–92.

Darlington, Y., Feeney, J.A. and Rixon, K. (2005) 'Practice challenges at the intersection of child protection and mental health', *Child and Family Social Work*, 10, pp 239–47.

DCSF (Department for Children, Schools and Families) (2010) *Working together to safeguard children: A guide to inter-agency working to safeguard and promote the welfare of children*, London: DCSF.

DfE (Department for Education) (2011) *A child-centred system: The government's response to the Munro Review of Child Protection*, London: The Stationery Office. Available at: www.education.gov.uk/publications.

DH (Department of Health) (2000) *Framework for the assessment of children in need and their families*, London: The Stationery Office.

DH (2010) *Equity and excellence: Liberating the NHS*, Cm 7881, London: The Stationery Office.

DH (2011a) *Government response to the NHS Future Forum report*, Cm 8113, London: The Stationery Office.

DH (2011b) *Safeguarding children in the reformed NHS: a co-produced work programme between the Department of Health, Department for Education, and national and local stakeholders*, London: The Stationery Office.

Diggins, M. (1999) 'Crossing over between services: the Lewisham experience', in A. Wier and A. Douglas (eds) *Child protection and mental health: Conflict of interest?*, Oxford: Butterworth Heinemann, pp 137–55.

Elgar, F.J. (2004) 'Mutual influences on maternal depression and child adjustment problems', *Clinical Psychology Review*, 24, pp 441–59.

Falkov, A. (1996) *Study of Working Together 'Part 8' reports*, London: DH,

Flynn, S. (2009) *Filicide: A literature review*, The National Confidential Inquiry into Suicide and Homicide by People with Mental Illness, Centre for Suicide Prevention, University of Manchester. Available at: www.medicine.manchester.ac.uk/mentalhealth/research/suicide/prevention/nci/reports/filicide_a_literatrue_review.pdf (accessed 16 October 2011).

Gammell, C. and Cockcroft, L. (2010) 'Starved girl Khyra Ishaq failed by social services', *The Telegraph* (online), 25 February. Available at: www.telegraph.co.uk/news/uknews/crime/7318878/Starved-girl-Khyra-Ishaq-failed-by-social-services.html (accessed 16 October 2011).

Glaser, D., Hall, A., Lindsey, C., Ramchandani, P. and Sturge, C. (2004) *Child abuse and neglect: The role of mental health services*, Council report CR120, London: Royal College of Psychiatrists.

Hetherington, R. and Baistow, K. (2001) 'Supporting families with a mentally ill parent: European perspectives on interagency cooperation', *Child Abuse Review*, 10, pp 351–65.

Japp K.P. and Kusche I. (2008) 'Systems theory and risk', in J.O. Zinn (ed) *Social theories of risk and uncertainty*, Oxford: Blackwell Publishing.

Johnson, K. (2009) 'Safeguarding children and mental health practice: experiencing the field', in L. Hughes and H. Owen (eds) *Good practice in safeguarding children: Working effectively in child protection*, London: Jessica Kingsley Publishers, pp 163–79.

Kaplan, C.A. (1999) 'The real risks children face: the role and perspective of the child psychiatrist', in A. Wier and A. Douglas (eds) *Child protection and mental health: Conflict of interest?*, Oxford: Butterworth Heinemann, pp 10–16.

London SCB (London Safeguarding Children Board) (2010) 'Serious case reviews in London'. Available at: www.londonscb.gov.uk/serious_case_reviews/ (accessed 16 October 2011).

Munro, E. (2011) *The Munro Review of Child Protection: Final report*, London: The Stationery Office. Available at: www.education.gov.uk/publications.

NCISH (National Confidential Inquiry into Suicide and Homicide by People with Mental Illness) (2006) Annual Figures (rev. 29 November).

NPSA (National Patient Safety Agency) (2009) *Preventing harm to children from parents with mental health needs* [rapid response report NPSA/2009/RRR003] 28 May. Available at: www.nrls.npsa.nhs.uk/resources/?entryid45=59898&p=5 (accessed 16 October 2011).

Ofsted (2008) *Learning lessons, taking action: Ofsted's evaluations of serious case reviews, 1 April 2007 to 31 March 2008*, Manchester: Office for Standards in Education, Children's Services and Skills.

Parker, E. (1999) 'Professional challenges and dilemmas', in A. Wier and A. Douglas (eds) *Child protection and mental health: Conflict of interest?*, Oxford: Butterworth Heinemann, pp 23–8.

Peake, A. and France, A. (2009) 'I'm glad my daughter's been named. Now she will feel fear like little Peter did', *The Sun* (online), 11 August. Available at: www.thesun.co.uk/sol/homepage/news/2580930/Baby-P-gran-welcomes-naming-and-shaming-of-her-daughter-and-boyfriend.html#ixzz0hyDZ7Zm4 (accessed 16 October 2011).

Reder, P. and Duncan, S. (1997) 'Adult psychiatry – a missing link in the child protection network: comments on Falkov's fatal child abuse and parental psychiatric disorder (DH, 1996)', *Child Abuse Review*, 6, pp 35–40.

Sayce, L. (1999) 'Parenting as a civil right: supporting service users who choose to have children', in A. Wier and A. Douglas (eds) *Child protection and mental health: Conflict of interest?*, Oxford: Butterworth Heinemann, pp 28–48.

SCIE (Social Care Institute for Excellence) (2009) *Think child, think parent, think family: A guide to parental mental health and child welfare*, SCIE guide 30. Available at: www.scie.org.uk/publications/guides/guide30/files/guide30.pdf (accessed 16 October 2011).

Smith, K., Coleman, K., Eder, S. and Hall, P. (eds) (2011) 'Homicides, firearm offences and intimate violence 2009/10', Home Office Statistical Bulletin 01/11.

Stanley, N., Penhale, B., Riordan, D., Barbour, R.S. and Holden, S. (2003) *Child protection and mental health services*, Bristol: The Policy Press.

Takei, T., Yamashita, H. and Yoshida, K. (2006) 'The mental health of mothers of physically abused children: the relationship with children's behavioural problems: report from Japan', *Child Abuse Review*, 15, pp 204–18.

The Daily Record (2010) 'Monster jailed over killing of Baby P loses appeal over rape of girl, age two' (online), 21 January. Available at: www.dailyrecord.co.uk/news/uk-world-news/2010/01/21/monster-jailed-over-killing-of-baby-p-loses-appeal-over-rape-of-girl-age-two-86908-21984541/ (accessed 16 October 2011).

Tunnard, J. (2004) 'Parental mental health problems: key messages from research, policy and practice', in *Research in practice*. Available at www.rep.org.uk.

Tye, C. and Precey, G. (1999) 'Building bridges: the interface between adult mental health and child protection', *Child Abuse Review*, 8, pp 164–71.

Warner, J. (2006) 'Inquiry reports as active texts and their function in relation to professional practice in mental health', *Health, Risk and Society*, 8(3), September, pp 223–37.

Wier, A. and Douglas, A. (eds) (1999) *Child protection and mental health: Conflict of interest?*, Oxford: Butterworth Heinemann.

FIVE

Adolescent-to-parent abuse and frontline service responses: does Munro matter?

Amanda Holt

> He'd just come in and he'd lost his temper with some kids outside, come in and just took it out on the house. Well, he actually picked me up and threw me across his bedroom as well and he's only 14 … and all they said to me was … the youth panel man turned round to the magistrates and said 'I think Mrs Smith should have a parenting order' and they just agreed straight away. But to me I was disgusted because it's me that got David arrested, hoping that he'd calm down, for when he gets older, sort of thing … I don't want him growing up and ending up in prison.
>
> (Lone mother of three, England)

Parent abuse is a hidden yet prevalent problem which presents a number of challenges to practitioners who work on the frontline in the fields of social care, criminal justice, education and health. Current practice struggles to meet these challenges and, as a consequence, families continue to be at risk. With the recent publication of the Munro Review (Munro, 2011), this chapter explores the extent to which it might enable better service responses for such vulnerable families. The chapter begins by outlining the defining characteristics of adolescent-to-parent abuse and explores why it presents distinct challenges to frontline practitioners who may nevertheless have considerable experience of working with other forms of family violence. In particular, this chapter discusses the tools that are currently available to practitioners who work in policing, youth justice, social care, education and health when faced with cases of parent abuse, and why such tools are inappropriate as a response. The chapter concludes by assessing how the key themes for change underpinning Munro's recommendations might enable the development of more appropriate statutory responses to parent abuse and highlights areas which require more fundamental consideration.

Adolescent-to-parent abuse: a challenge to frontline services

Parent abuse has not yet achieved the status of 'social problem' which other forms of family abuse have, such as child abuse, intimate partner violence (IPV) and elder abuse. Nevertheless, it shares a number of important features. It is characterised by a persistent pattern of behaviour[1] which uses physical, emotional or economic means to practise power and exert control over a parent, and it may involve shouting and screaming, blackmail, threats, demands and insults, and/or physical violence. Its impact can be profound: research has been relatively consistent in finding feelings of fear, guilt, shame and despair in parents and feelings of helplessness and inadequacy in the child or young person. Relations with other family members are likely to be strained and – as with other forms of family abuse – it has been implicated in damage to physical and mental health. It can also disrupt the employment, educational and financial stability of individuals and families. While the hidden nature of parent abuse inevitably makes measuring its prevalence difficult, research in both the UK and elsewhere estimates that it features in 5–15% of families (for a review, see Holt, in press).

Like other forms of family abuse, parent abuse is often characterised by a gendered dynamic: mothers are far more likely to report victimisation and sons are slightly more likely to act as perpetrators. It is also linked to other forms of family abuse, in that it often features in families where there is a history of IPV (Boxer et al, 2009; Kennedy et al, 2010), and it has been found to co-occur in families where there is parent-to-child abuse (Brezina, 1999; Ullman and Strauss, 2003). Siblings are also likely to be victims of the perpetrating child (Laurent and Derry, 1999) and there is some evidence that young people perpetrating parent abuse are more likely subsequently to develop abusive behaviours towards dating partners (LaPorte et al, 2011).

However, despite similarities with other forms of family abuse, there are a number of characteristics that set parent abuse apart and make it a particular challenge to frontline practitioners who work with children and families. First, it takes place within a very specific discursive context where parents, and particularly mothers, are routinely 'blamed' for the alleged wrongdoings of their children. Such discourses of parent blame are culturally reproduced through a range of institutions, but they have taken a very distinct form over the past 15 years through political rhetoric concerning youth crime and the invocation of the notion of a 'parenting deficit' (Goldson and Jamieson, 2002). This has culminated in the implementation of parental responsibility laws, such as those which enable courts to issue parenting orders in cases where young people offend or are deemed at risk of doing so. Cases have been recorded of parenting orders being issued to parents as a result of their victimisation by their son/daughter (see Holt, 2009); the challenge to the statutory services, which must then work with these parents (who, as the opening quote highlights, feel they have been 'punished' for their own victimisation), cannot be underestimated. Second, parent abuse involves an inversion of how we normatively conceptualise power relations between parents and their children. While children are variously constructed as 'innocent', 'at risk' and 'dependent' (James and James, 2004), parents are constructed *in relation to* children, and therefore notions that parents are 'responsible', 'safe' and 'self-determined' permeate and shape the configuration of *all* statutory services which work with them. The existence of parent abuse challenges these conceptions.

In part, it is this unsettling characteristic of parent abuse that makes it so hidden, as parents often feel ashamed and guilty about what is happening, and consequently find it difficult to come forward and seek support. Such silence is mirrored in the policy landscape, and the lack of any statutory practice guidance means that frontline services are unable to respond to parent abuse appropriately or consistently. Given Munro's criticism that current statutory guidance in relation to child protection is *so extensive* that it limits the effectiveness of practitioner responses, the lack of any statutory guidance in relation to family protection is particularly conspicuous. To illustrate the consequences of this policy silence, the following section discusses the ways in which frontline services are currently equipped to deal with adolescent-to-parent abuse when cases arise, with specific reference to policing, youth offending services, children and adult social care, and education and health services.

Current statutory responses to adolescent-to-parent abuse

Criminal justice responses to parent abuse

Parents may contact the police directly to report a violent incident, or cases may be referred to the police from other services. Often parents report that they contact the police because they want to send a message to their child that their behaviour is unacceptable – perhaps through the police giving their child 'a good talking to'. However, research that has sought parents' accounts of parent abuse, including their experiences of seeking help, suggests that this rarely happens (Edenborough et al, 2008; Holt, 2009, 2011). More frequently, parents report feeling that parent abuse is not taken seriously by the police (Cottrell, 2001; Edenborough et al, 2008; Haw, 2010; Holt, 2011) and that police intervention is counterproductive in sending a message to the child/young person that they are immune from formal sanctions (Tew and Nixon, 2010). Other parents have reported feeling blamed by the police, resulting in a reluctance to make any further contact (Cottrell and Monk, 2004; Haw, 2010). Fear also produces a barrier to parents seeking police support: parents fear that they themselves may be charged with an offence (a fear which is often exacerbated by their child's threats that they will make a complaint) (Eckstein, 2004). They may also fear being subjected to institutionalised discrimination based on 'race', sexuality or social class (Cottrell, 2001).

Unlike cases of other forms of family violence, individual police forces do not generally utilise a specific 'category code' to monitor incidents of parent abuse, and there is no existing police guidance on how to respond to such incidents. Therefore the tools available to the police are very limited beyond arresting the young person for a criminal offence (if they are over 10 years old). Furthermore, while a range of referral tools are available to the police in cases of child abuse, IPV and elder abuse (such as notification to child protection services in cases of suspected child abuse or referral to a monthly multi-agency risk assessment conference (MARAC) in cases of IPV), there is no policy or practice guidance available when the perpetrator is a minor and the victim is an adult. While there is evidence that MARACs have been used in very serious cases of assault against parents, the options available are extremely limited when it comes to working with a person under 18 years because MARACs' aim is to safeguard the victim and this cannot be done meaningfully when the 'perpetrator' is living in the same home as the 'victim' and is under their care. Because many parents will resist their child being arrested, and many more will resist testifying in court against them, there is often no official 'case', no 'lead contact' and nowhere to refer the parent. The next time a parent contacts police for help, the process will therefore start again, with different personnel offering a different level of service and different advice.

For youth offending services, parent abuse is likely to be brought to the attention of practitioners when they begin working with young people as a result of their involvement in other offences. Again, with no assessment tools available to help identify parent abuse, cases tend to be recognised inadvertently through observation or parent disclosure. The tools to enable youth offending services to respond appropriately to parent abuse are very limited, since the service is set up on the assumption that youth offending takes place *outside* the family home and the root of youth offending is situated *within the family*. Thus many post-sentence interventions for young people, such as fines, community reparation or home curfews, are wholly inappropriate for cases of parent abuse and are likely either to have no impact on family life or, worse still, enable further damage to already strained family relations. Similarly damaging is the use of parenting orders, which force victims to attend parenting programmes to make them 'take responsibility' for the crimes of their child, which may intensify already existing feelings of resentment and shame (Holt, 2009).

However, beyond this rather punitive and parent-blaming youth justice framework, there are signs that local youth offending teams

– in collaboration with other agencies – are developing their own intervention programmes specifically designed for work with parent abuse. For example, Break4Change was developed by Brighton and Hove youth offending team in collaboration with the targeted youth support service, RISE (a local domestic violence support service), the family intervention project and the local CAMHS. It is also worth exploring overseas developments, such as the use of restorative justice, which was piloted successfully in Canada and Australia (see Doran, 2007; Daly and Nancarrow, 2009). However, one challenge to such developments is the more fundamental question of whether a criminal justice response, which might usefully alleviate abuse in the short term (or at least send a strong message as to its unacceptability), is ultimately in the best interests of a child and his/her family in the longer term.

Local authority social services' responses to parent abuse

If criminal justice frameworks struggle to accommodate the problem of parent abuse because they are premised on the notion that parents are *responsible* for youth offending, then social care frameworks face a similar conundrum in that they operate according to the principle that children and young people are *vulnerable* and are therefore in need of safeguarding from potential (adult) perpetrators of abuse and violence – particularly adults who bear caregiving responsibilities. In terms of children's social care, research suggests that practitioners who come across parent abuse struggle to reconcile these professional orientations with the notion that it is *a child* who is perpetrating violence against an *adult victim* (Nixon, in press). Nixon (in press) also found such assumptions evident in social work practitioners' explanations of parent abuse, which particularly drew on notions of a 'parenting deficit'. Indeed, research has found social workers to be unfamiliar with the term 'parent abuse' and reluctant to use the term when talking about children, preferring the terms 'challenging behaviour' or 'poor parenting', for example (Hunter et al, 2010; Nixon, in press). That inappropriate responses can flow from this is powerfully highlighted in a case recounted to Nixon (in press) where a mother who had threatened to leave the family home due to violence from her son was threatened by social services with prosecution for child abandonment.

As stipulated by the 1989 Children Act, there are two levels of threshold that need to be met to instigate an intervention from children's social care: first, a risk of 'significant harm', where there is 'ill treatment or impairment of health or development' (Children Act 1989, s 47); and second, where a child is 'in need' if they are not achieving or maintaining 'a reasonable standard of health or development' (Children Act 1989, s 17). At the highest threshold, a care order or a supervision order may be made when a child is 'beyond parental control' (s 31) – a term which one could argue epitomises the parent abuse dynamic. Certainly, in some cases, the child him/herself may be experiencing ongoing abuse and a child protection response may be appropriate. It may also be appropriate if a child is sexually abusing their parent, although such cases are very rare. However, in most other cases, the perpetrating child is unlikely to pass this threshold. If siblings are also being victimised, they may reach the necessary harm threshold, but sibling abuse is often minimised both within professional discourses (Phillips et al, 2009) and among families themselves (Kettry and Emery, 2006).

If the child meets the lower threshold, a range of family support services should be provided. These might include respite care, financial support, transport assistance, and advice and counselling. However, the scant evidence that exists suggests that parents do not receive such services, despite direct and repeated requests for help (Parentline Plus, 2008; Holt, 2009, 2011; Hunter et al, 2010; Nixon, in press). There may also be barriers preventing some parents from seeking support from social care services, the most pertinent being parents' fear that their child (and their siblings) may be taken into care – a fear which has been documented in relation to parents' fears of social care involvement in cases of IPV (Stanley et al, 2009) and suspected child abuse (Cleaver and Freeman, 1995). However, it is important to recognise that, given the found links between parent abuse and earlier abuses in the family, the young people involved in parent abuse may be already known to social services, perhaps pointing the way to how social care services might be involved in a larger public policy agenda to combat the problem of parent abuse.

Of course, social care services also include adult social care, and this may be another avenue where parents might receive support if experiencing parent abuse. Indeed, the policy guidance document *Safeguarding adults* states that 'all citizens should have access to relevant services for addressing issues of abuse and neglect' (ADASS, 2005: 4) and cites article 2 (Right to life), article 3 (Freedom from torture) and article 8 (Right to family life) from the 1998 Human Rights Act in support of this access. However, the policy guidance that follows makes it clear that only adults considered to be 'at risk' are qualified to receive the multi-agency response which is set out in the document, defined as adults who 'may be eligible for community care services [and] unable to protect [themselves]' (ADASS, 2005: 4). And while the document recognises that practitioners also have a public duty to those adults *not* covered by the policy guidance (ADASS, 2005: 5), demands on resources and a lack of policy guidance for those adults who are *not* normatively constructed as 'at risk' means this is not being realised in practice.

Education and health services' responses to parent abuse

A recent study by Parentline Plus (2010) concerning parents' attempts to seek support for their aggressive children found that schools and GPs were most frequently contacted by parents, with help also sought from educational psychologists, health visitors, psychiatrists and CAMHS. However, the little research that exists suggests that parents received little support from either (Holt, 2011). In terms of frontline responses, any practitioner working with children and young people is likely to be directed by the child protection procedural guidance produced by their local safeguarding children board (LSCB). To take one example, the London Safeguarding Children Board (London SCB, 2010) guidance recognises that 'children of both genders can direct physical, sexual or emotional violence towards their parents, siblings and/or partner' (s 5.20.2). And although the rest of this section is oriented (and worded) towards 'other children' as the potential victims, referral and assessment is recommended when there is an allegation or suspicion of physical and/or emotional abuse or harm towards 'another child *or adult*' (SCB, 2010, s 5.20.6, emphasis added). The guidance states that practitioner responses should involve discussion with the organisation's manager and nominated safeguarding children adviser, whereby a common assessment (CAF) may take place (which may include the identification of a 'lead professional' and the delivery of a CAF action plan) before deciding whether to refer the case on to the local authority children's social care department. Similar guidance is recommended in *Safeguarding children affected by gang activity and/or serious youth violence for child practitioners* (London SCB, 2009), which points out that children and young people who perpetrate violence may need to be recognised as 'both … victim and … perpetrator' (p 15). Thus the guidance suggests a two-pronged approach where professionals must assess and support the child/young person's welfare and wellbeing at the same time as responding 'in a criminal justice capacity' (s 6.1.2). However, this document fails to identify violence against parents in the home as a particular issue, where responding 'in a criminal justice capacity' may be more complex.

Each LSCB also provides guidance for practitioners when there is suspected domestic violence in the home, and this may also be relevant to those working with children and young people. For example, *Safeguarding children abused through domestic violence* (London SCB, 2008) suggests that practitioners should assess the risk to both the mother (using the CAADArisk identification checklist) and to each child in the family home (using DVRIM) and then decide whether to refer the case to children's social care services for further assessment. Contact may also be made with the mother (if the violence is disclosed by another person), and safety plans can be developed. However, despite such guidance, concerns have been raised in particular about health professionals' responses to domestic violence and a number of strategies are under development concerning how primary care trusts (PCTs) and their partners can better identify and respond to suspected cases of domestic violence (DH, 2010). Furthermore, Munro raised her own concerns regarding the potential sidelining of safeguarding practices in the midst of ongoing health reform. Overall, this provides little assurance that current health sector responses to adolescent-to-parent abuse are adequate.

Meeting the challenges of adolescent-to-parent abuse: does Munro matter?

The Munro Review (Munro, 2011), and the government response to it, suggests that child protection requires a 'child-centred system' and Munro's 15 recommendations draw on a number of overarching themes which should underpin the future practice of services which come into contact with children, young people and their families. Given the current policy silence surrounding parent abuse, and its devastating effects when left unchecked, this would seem like an ideal opportunity to develop frontline practice in a way that recognises parent abuse and enables a more adequate service response than the one we have at present. The following section draws on a number of overarching themes for change that underpin the Munro Review to discuss their potential in achieving this goal.

Community-based multi-agency working

Munro's review emphasises the importance of community-based multi-agency services in providing early intervention to children and families most in need. However, as this chapter has discussed, parent abuse presents particular challenges for multi-agency working. For a start, cases are not brought to statutory services' attention through any one pathway: the report by Parentline Plus (2010) found that parents are likely to seek help from more than one of a range of services (including criminal justice, social care, education and health). Therefore we need a common framework to enable different agencies to identify, monitor and respond to parent abuse consistently to ensure that parents are not continually referred on to different agencies without end, as is presently the case. This should also enable us to begin measuring its prevalence and characteristics in particular local contexts, and enable the emergence of practitioner expertise on what kind of responses work best. At the very least, we need to develop a category code so that incidents of 'parent abuse' can be flagged up, enabled by a clear definition and assessment tool which all statutory bodies can work with. Furthermore, given the complexity of parent abuse, it is clear that a number of agencies need to be involved in the response, since the agency most appropriate to deal with the 'perpetrator' may not necessarily be the one most suitable to respond to the 'victim' or other family members. Furthermore, different responses may be required depending on the form and severity of the abuse. However, one particular service does need to provide a single point of contact to follow a case through. If this doesn't happen, cases may be left to drop, leaving parents lost and practitioners not knowing the outcome of a referral and whether it worked or not. This means that the development of professional knowledge – something encouraged by Munro – would be severely hampered.

Early intervention and an 'early help offer'

Munro's emphasis on early intervention provided collaboratively by statutory, voluntary and community organisations includes the suggestion of an 'early help offer' in cases where families' needs 'do not meet the criteria for receiving children's social care services' (Munro, 2011: 78). This seems particularly relevant in cases of parent abuse where, as we have discussed, the family do not meet the criteria for support from social services, nor from any other statutory service. Other voluntary and community organisations, such as victim support, domestic violence organisations and parenting support organisations, frequently receive requests for help for parent abuse but, as is the case in the statutory sector, they are configured in ways that construct the parent and child within normative victim/perpetrator demarcations, which can make responses (such as a women's refuge) inappropriate. It is clear that something beyond existing community/voluntary support will be needed to support the statutory sector in its response to parent abuse, although the Munro Review – and the government response to it – says little about the future roles of the voluntary and community sectors, or how they will be resourced.

A shift from a 'compliance culture' to a 'learning culture'

Munro highlights the limits to what an over-bureaucratic system can achieve and calls for less centralised prescription and greater decision-making freedom for frontline practitioners. To inform this decision-making, Munro emphasises the need for national dissemination of good practice, with training and accreditation where relevant. In relation to parent abuse, there is some good practice already emerging within youth offending services, but at present these are developed locally and there is no requirement for nationally accredited standardised services as for adult intervention programmes. This means that other practitioners inside and outside the youth justice field cannot easily learn from them, and youth courts may not necessarily be aware of their existence when faced with a case concerning parent abuse. Therefore, while Munro emphasises the principle of local authorities developing practices appropriate to local need, there is a risk that programmes that have recently emerged to respond to parent abuse – which are still in their infancy and remain unevaluated – remain hidden from other local authorities which may benefit from them. A resource for sharing best practice across different sectors, as well as to map what is available regionally to enable appropriate referrals to be made, is therefore essential. It is also worth highlighting that while youth offending services appear to be at the forefront of developing such programmes, they may not be the most appropriate arena for delivering them. Finally, part of the 'learning culture' advocated by Munro might also include raising awareness of practitioners' own potential professional 'blindspots', which can produce unhelpful responses (such as youth courts issuing sentences which further damage the parent, or social workers assuming that 'poor parenting' is a *cause* of – rather than a potential *consequence* of – parent abuse).

Emphasis on the child's journey

Given the links between parent abuse and child abuse, IPV and sibling abuse, it is clear that parent abuse needs to be understood in the wider context of family violence. In many cases, the perpetrating child or young person will also be, or will have been, a victim of family violence. Therefore Munro's emphasis on a 'whole system' approach to understanding child protection, rather than the current atomism which focuses on isolated problems and individual error, is to be welcomed. However, parents, and particularly mothers, may be experiencing *revictimisation* which is likely to have particularly profound effects on their mental, physical and emotional health, including their confidence to parent effectively. Therefore, while the emphasis on the child's journey in Munro's review is necessary to enable an analysis of the complex trajectories undoubtedly involved in parent abuse, the voice and needs of parents must not be marginalised.

As this chapter has outlined, the Munro Review has the potential to provide a 'watershed moment' in raising awareness of the prevalence and problems produced by adolescent-to-parent abuse, and in enabling the development of agreed strategies on how frontline services might better respond. As Hunter et al (2010) suggest, the construction of a social problem determines how policy frameworks emerge, and it is clear that we are not yet decided on what kind of problem (and whose problem) adolescent-to-parent abuse is. Such questions are clearly more fundamental than those raised by the Munro Review, but now, while the government highlights the need to consider Munro's recommendations 'in the round', perhaps the circle of discussion could be enlarged to provide room for this important debate.

Note

[1] It is important to recognise that parent abuse goes beyond 'one-off' incidents or the everyday experiences of children 'hitting out' at parents, which can happen for all sorts of medical, developmental and situational reasons.

References

ADASS (Association of Directors of Adult Social Services) (2005) *Safeguarding adults: A national framework of standards for good practice and outcomes in adult protection work* [online]. Available at: www.adass.org.uk/old/publications/guidance/safeguarding.pdf (accessed 13 September 2011).

Boxer, P., Gullan, R.L. and Mahoney, A. (2009) 'Adolescents' physical aggression towards parents in a clinically referred sample', *Journal of Clinical Child and Adolescent Psychology*, 38, pp 106–16.

Brezina, T. (1999) 'Teenage violence toward parents as an adaptation to family strain', *Youth and Society*, 30(4), pp 416–44.

Cleaver, H. and Freeman, P. (1995) *Parental perspectives in cases of suspected child abuse*, London: HMSO.

Cottrell, B. (2001) *Parent abuse: The abuse of parents by their teenage children*, Ottawa: Family Violence Prevention Unit, Health Canada.

Cottrell, B. and Monk, P. (2004) 'Adolescent to parent abuse', *Journal of Family Issues*, 25, pp 1072–95.

Daly, M. and Nancarrow, H. (2009) 'Restorative justice and youth violence towards parents', in J. Ptacek (ed) *Restorative justice and violence against women*, Oxford: Oxford University Press, pp 150–76.

DH (Department of Health) (2010) *Responding to violence against women and children – the role of the NHS: The report of the Taskforce on the Health Aspects of Violence Against Women and Children* (March), London: DH. Available at: www.dh.gov.uk/prod_consum_dh/groups/dh_digitalassets/@dh/@en/@ps/documents/digitalasset/dh_113824.pdf (accessed 6 September 2011).

Doran, J.E. (2007) *Restorative justice and family violence: Youth-to-parent abuse* (unpublished MA), Mount Saint Vincent University.

Eckstein, N.J. (2004) 'Emergent issues in families experiencing adolescent-to-parent abuse', *Western Journal of Communication*, 68(4), pp 365–88.

Edenborough, M.D., Jackson, D., Mannix, J. and Wilkes, L. (2008) 'Living in the red zone: the experience of child-to-mother violence', *Child and Family Social Work*, 13, pp 464–73.

Goldson, B. and Jamieson, J. (2002) 'Youth crime, the "parenting deficit" and state intervention: a contextual critique', *Youth Justice*, 2(2), pp 92–9.

Haw, A. (2010) *Parenting over violence: Understanding and empowering mothers affected by adolescent violence in the home*, Perth, Australia: Patricia Giles Centre.

Holt, A. (2009) 'Parent abuse: some reflections on the adequacy of a youth justice response', *Internet Journal of Criminology*, November, pp 1–11. Available at: www.internetjournalofcriminology.com/Holt_Parent_Abuse_Nov_09.pdf (accessed 16 October 2011).

Holt, A. (2011) '"The terrorist in my home": teenagers' violence towards parents – constructions of parent experiences in public online message boards', *Child & Family Social Work*, 16(4), pp 454–63.

Holt, A. (in press) 'Researching parent abuse: a critical review of the methods', *Social Policy and Society*, 11(2).

Hunter, C., Nixon, J. and Parr, S. (2010) 'Mother abuse: a matter of youth justice, child welfare or domestic violence?', *Journal of Law and Society,* 37(2), pp 264–84.

James, A. and James, A.L. (2004) *Reconstructing childhood*, Basingstoke: Palgrave.

Kennedy, T.D, Edmonds, W.A., Dann, K.T.J. and Burnett, K.F. (2010) 'The clinical and adaptive features of young offenders with histories of child–parent violence', *Journal of Family Violence*, 25(5), pp 509–20.

Kettrey, H. and Emery, B. (2006) 'The discourse of sibling violence', *Journal of Family Violence*, 21, pp 407–16.

LaPorte, L., Depeng, J., Pepler, D.J. and Chamberland, C. (2011) 'The relationship between adolescents' experience of family violence and dating violence', *Youth and Society*, 42(1), pp 3–27.

Laurent, A. and Derry, A. (1999) 'Violence of French adolescents toward their parents: characteristics and contexts', *Journal of Adolescent Health*, 25(1), pp 21–6.

London SCB (London Safeguarding Children Board) (2008) *Safeguarding children abused through domestic violence* (March) (online). Available at: www.londonscb.gov.uk/domestic_violence/ (accessed 13 September 2011).

London SCB (2009) *Safeguarding children affected by gang activity and/ or serious youth violence for child practitioners* (November) [online]. Available at: www.londonscb.gov.uk (accessed 13 September 2011).

London SCB (2010) *London child protection procedures* (December) (online). Available at: www.londonscb.gov.uk/procedures (accessed 16 October 2011).

Munro, E. (2011) *The Munro Review of Child Protection: Final report*, London: The Stationery Office. Available at: www.education.gov.uk/publications.

Nixon, J. (in press) 'Practitioners' constructions of parent abuse', *Social Policy and Society*, 11(2).

Parentline Plus (2008) 'You can't say go and sit on the naughty step because they turn round and say make me', *Aggressive behaviour in children: Parents' experiences and needs* (online). Available at: http://plptesting.tribalhosted.co.uk/default.aspx?page=viewarticle&module=articles-view&id=309 (accessed 13 September 2011).

Parentline Plus (2010) *When family life hurts: Family experience of aggression in children*, London: Parentline Plus.

Phillips, D.A., Phillips, K.H., Grupp, K. and Trigg, L. (2009) 'Sibling violence silenced: rivalry, competition, wrestling, playing, roughhousing, benign', *Advances in Nursing Science*, 32(2), E1-E16.

Stanley, N., Cleaver, H. and Hart, D. (2009) 'The impact of domestic violence, parental mental health problems, substance misuse and learning disability on parenting capacity', in J. Horwath (ed) *The child's world: The comprehensive guide to assessing children in need* (2nd edn), London: Jessica Kingsley.

Tew, J. and Nixon, J. (2010) 'Parent abuse: opening up a discussion of a complex instance of family power relations', *Social Policy & Society*, 9(4), pp 579–89.

Ulman, A. and Straus, M.A. (2003) 'Violence by children against mothers in relation to violence between parents and corporal punishment by parents', *Journal of Comparative Family Studies*, 34(1), pp 41–60.

SIX

Older children and the child protection system

Gwyther Rees and Mike Stein

Child protection of young people aged 11 to 17 is a surprisingly unexplored issue. In this chapter we review two recent research studies in England that aimed to address this gap. We present the key findings from these projects and consider their implications in the light of the Munro Review of Child Protection and the government's response.

The Munro Review itself acknowledges some of the potentially distinctive aspects of child protection issues in relation to this particular age group (Munro, 2011: s 2.30, p 37). The government's response also contains specific acknowledgement of this issue:

> Children in all age groups can be vulnerable so it is important that ... services also address the needs of older children to provide a timely offer of help to teenagers. The importance of early help for this age group is as vital as it is for young children. (DfE, 2011: 9)

We will discuss the relevance of some of the key themes emerging from the government's response to the Munro Review when considering how to meet the protective needs of young people aged 11 to 17 who may be experiencing maltreatment.[1]

Young people aged 11 to 17 and the child protection system in England

Almost a quarter of all children who become the subject of a child protection plan in England are aged between 10 and 15 years old. It is also notable that, as for younger children, neglect remains the most common category of maltreatment, even among this older age group. Given their developmental stage, maltreated young people in this age group will often face different issues and require different responses than younger children. In fact, age-related considerations can affect definitions of what constitutes 'maltreatment' – for example, levels of parental supervision that would be deemed extremely neglectful in relation to a very young child would be regarded as normative parenting of an older teenager. Yet, until recently, the specific issues faced by older young people, and the professionals working with them, have not been a prominent theme within child protection research, policy and practice.

Part of the reason for the neglect of this issue may stem from the way the child protection system has developed in England over the past few decades. The government's response to the Munro Review notes:

> Over the years, individual child tragedies have prompted national reviews and inquiries, resulting in calls for action. In response, legislation has been passed; rulebooks have expanded; more procedures and processes have been introduced and structures have been changed. But the fundamental problems have not gone away. (DfE, 2011: 2)

This view of the recent evolution of the child protection system is particularly pertinent to older young people because most of the tragedies alluded to in the quote above relate to children of primary school age or younger.[2] To the extent that developments in policy and practice have been influenced by the aim of preventing similar tragedies, there is a risk that they may fail to address the most important issues for older young people and may in fact distort the workings of the child protection system.

There has recently been evidence of the vulnerability of older young people who are maltreated. Two analyses of serious case reviews (SCRs) involving death or serious harm to a child or young person (Brandon et al, 2008, 2009) have found that between a fifth and a quarter of such reviews involved young people aged 11 to 17 years old at the time of the incident. This recognition has sparked renewed concern about the provision of preventative and protective interventions for this age group.

Recent research on young people and the child protection system

In this section we discuss some of the key themes that have emerged from two recent studies that we undertook jointly (with colleagues)[3] on specific issues relating to the child protection of young people aged 11 to 17 in England.

The first of these studies, which focused on issues of neglect for this age group, was funded by the (then) DCSF as part of the Safeguarding Research Initiative. The project was based on a literature review and consultations with young people and professionals. Outputs were a summary literature review (Stein et al, 2009), a guide for young people[4] and a multi-agency guide for professionals (Hicks and Stein, 2010). These components also formed the basis of a book on neglected adolescents (Rees et al, 2011).

We draw more fully on a second study, funded by the Lottery, which explored initial responses to potential issues of maltreatment of young people aged 11 to 17 by children's social care and a range of referring agencies (Rees et al, 2010). It included a literature review, interviews with young people and professionals, a survey of professionals, and an analysis of recent policy.

Previous international research evidence

The reviews of international literature undertaken for both the above studies identified a range of evidence but also some significant gaps in knowledge about the issue.

While a lot is known about the general background risk and protective factors which affect the likelihood of a child or young person being maltreated, very little is known specifically about the factors for this age group. On the other hand, there is quite a lot of evidence about the consequences of maltreatment for this age group. Some of this comes from studies of parenting style and specifically focuses on the relative outcomes of authoritative, authoritarian, permissive and neglectful styles. Within this framework there is substantial evidence that the neglectful parenting style (characterised by a combination of low warmth and low control/demandingness) is associated with a range of negative outcomes for this age group, including poor mental health and wellbeing, risky health behaviours, poor academic achievement, antisocial behaviour, and offending.

A second source of information about age-related patterns in outcomes associated with maltreatment comes from the Rochester Youth Development Study, a longitudinal study of young people in the US (Thornberry et al, 2001; Smith et al, 2005; Thornberry et al, 2010). The findings of this study suggest that young people who experience maltreatment only during adolescence display a range of negative outcomes at least as strong as those of children who experience maltreatment only during earlier childhood. The study also highlights some of the distinctive potential outcomes of maltreatment experienced in the teenage years, including increased risks of 'externalising' behaviours such as offending, substance use and other health-risking behaviours. Other studies (Sternberg et al, 2005; Stewart et al, 2008) have produced similar evidence of differences in outcomes depending on the timing of experience of maltreatment.

The international research also carries some important messages about professional judgement and decision-making in child protection services in relation to children and young people of different ages. A number of studies have used hypothetical vignettes to explore the effects of the age of children on assessments made by professionals and the general public. Many, though not all, of these studies (for example, Collings and Payne, 1991; Zellman, 1992; Maynard and Wiederman, 1997; Webster et al, 2005; Rogers and Davies, 2007) suggest that older young people in scenarios of potential child protection concern are more likely to be attributed with some blame for the maltreatment and are less likely be seen as 'at risk' and to be referred or considered for child protection interventions.

On the same topic, a study of assessments made by professionals and young people of the extent and severity of maltreatment (McGee et al, 1995) found a lack of concordance between professionals' and young people's assessments. It also indicated that young people's own assessments may be at least as accurate as those of professionals in terms of predicting the longer-term outcomes of maltreatment. A more recent study (Everson et al, 2008) generated similar findings. These studies therefore draw attention to the importance of listening to the views and experiences of young people in the child protection system.

Findings from our research with professionals

Moving on to the findings from the data gathered from professionals and agencies for our study, the overall picture was one of uncertainty and diversity in response to the needs of older young people who may be experiencing maltreatment, with resource considerations forming an important backdrop to decision-making.

Statistics on the processing of referrals in four local authority areas participating in the study highlighted some substantial age-related variations in the way child protection processes were implemented. Although there were some differences in patterns between the four areas, there was a broadly consistent picture that cases involving older young people were less likely to advance through the various milestones of the system than those involving younger children. So cases relating to older young people were less likely to receive an initial assessment, less likely to receive a core assessment, less likely to become the subject of a section 47 enquiry and less likely to result in a child protection plan being formulated.

However, this did not necessarily mean that older young people were not receiving appropriate services. First, this analysis related to all requests for a service and it may have been that a higher proportion of referrals of older young people did not relate to issues of maltreatment (although, as we shall see, there are issues about age-related assessment and decision-making). Second, there are some indications that older young people may be more likely to be subject to a child in need review. This suggests that older young people may be following different routes through the processes and services implemented by children's social care departments.

The surveys and interviews undertaken with professionals from referring agencies and children's social care services shed light on a number of factors which led to these age-related patterns. The first factor was evidence of age-related variations in professional assessments of risk. A vignettes-based survey of referring professionals (in schools, the police, youth justice services and the voluntary sector) suggested that, given the same scenario, professionals viewed the likely long-term consequences of maltreatment to be less serious when the age of the child or young person in the scenario was greater. A key theme emerging from this research was the concept that older young people are more 'resilient' to maltreatment, as the following quotes from a senior manager and from a practitioner in children's social care illustrate: 'more resilient as they get older so the impact of that abuse might not be as significant' (senior manager); 'They are older, deemed not as "vulnerable" as babies/younger children' (social work practitioner) (Rees et al, 2010: 148).

As already discussed, this notion of the increased resilience of older young people is not necessarily borne out by the research evidence, which suggests a much more complex and unclear picture of the relative consequences of maltreatment experienced at different ages. This includes evidence of increased risk for older young people in some outcome areas.

In addition to this theme of resilience, some professionals saw older young people as being more competent to escape maltreatment and to seek help, and this also lowered perceptions of risk. However, as discussed later, this factor does not necessarily mean that young people will in reality seek help.

So, to some extent, referring professionals were less likely to make referrals of older children owing to lower assessments of risk. However, there were other factors related to the workings of the child protection system which also appeared to deter referrals. Some professionals indicated that their doubts about whether to make a referral were influenced by their perceptions of the likelihood of children's social care taking action. There was a recognition among referring professionals of the very high demands on resources within statutory child protection, and a belief that action would not be taken through this route. The following quote is from a potential referring professional in relation to a scenario of supervisory neglect of a 15-year-old male:

> There appears to be no boundaries or parental guidance for this child, therefore making him vulnerable. I believe he is more likely to become involved in crime and substance misuse. (However, given his age and children services workload, I do not believe this would be actioned, sorry to say this.) I would make a child in need referral as opposed to a child protection referral. (Rees et al, 2010: 85)

This view was supported by material from some of the interviews with children's social care professionals:

> **Interviewer**: Ok, what do you see as the biggest challenges you face in terms of providing protective services for older children?
>
> **Social work practitioner**: Prioritising them. That's got to be it. You know, we are an understaffed team with, you know, worked to the hilt, staff here don't just don't have a second in the day at all to take a breather and we can't, we can't rush out to a 16-year-old who's perhaps sofa-surfing and perhaps experimenting with drugs and getting into crime, you know that's a big worry, but we can't prioritise that when we're working with 0 to 5 year olds in, you know, some pretty dire situations.
> (Rees et al, 2010: 136)

For referring professionals, their views on the likelihood of child protection action influenced their decision about referral because there were also perceived negative consequences of making a referral. For example, some teachers in the study expressed concern about damage to relationships with parents. It would appear therefore that there is a risk of a negative reinforcing cycle, where perceptions of high thresholds for this age group deter the likelihood of professionals making referrals.

A final key theme from interviews with practitioners, managers and policymakers in this study was a sense that the current child protection system and processes were not the most appropriate or effective way of meeting the needs of young people aged 11 to 17 who were experiencing maltreatment. There were a number of reasons for this, including a view that the system did not recognise older young people's need for choice and control; the reluctance of young people to engage with social work professionals; and a belief that child protection plans were often difficult to put into practice with parents of older young people:

> I think the child protection system as we know it … is fine … robust … but it's more geared towards children and young babies in my view and it doesn't necessarily take account of the more complex sets of issues around adolescents, because the child in child protection is a very passive participant in the whole process. (Rees et al, 2010: 149)

As a result of these concerns, it appeared that a number of local authority areas involved in the study had developed alternative approaches to trying to meet the needs of older young people who were being maltreated. These included using the child in need process rather than the child protection process and developing multi-agency approaches to risk assessment and management. It may be that this divergence of approaches is one of the explanations for the wide variations in proportions of older young people becoming subject to child protection plans in different local authority areas in England (as noted in Rees et al, 2010).

While the rationale for this diversity of approaches is clear, our study noted that, at this stage, there is a lack of evidence of what works best in relation to the different approaches in operation in different areas. There appears to be considerable scope for efforts to extract and share learning from these local variations in practice.

Young people's views

The research described here also included 24 interviews with young people with experience of the child protection system.[5] These interviews indicated the potential for effective social work interventions with this age group when an effective working relationship is developed:

> She's really … I've still got her now, she's really, really nice. … Like she's really easy to talk to and really chatty. She's a lot more helpful than the first one, like I've had regular meetings with her, and we've done like mind maps of family and like putting people who are closer in the inner circles and stuff like that.
>
> (Young person aged 17, in Rees et al, 2010: 52)

On the other hand, the interviews highlighted some key barriers to young people seeking help and to young people engaging successfully with professionals. In terms of accessing help, the first obstacle faced by young people was often a lack of awareness of the helping services available and how to access them. This finding has been found in previous research (for example, Featherstone and Evans, 2004; Gorin, 2004; Rees et al, 2009). In addition to this practical barrier, other factors come into play. Young people described being concerned about the potential consequences of disclosing abuse, for themselves and for other members of their family including the abuser:

> Cos me and my mum used to cover it up. I used to have bruises, the lot, and we just used to make up stories and just … so at the same time it's what the child wants to tell you and it's what the parent wants to tell you. Because things can easily get covered up. Because I've done it many a time before and that's only purely because I was so loyal to my mum and I thought social services were the bad ones.
>
> (Young person aged 17, in Rees et al, 2010: 43)

These concerns were exacerbated by doubts about trust and confidentiality in relation to helping professionals. There are thus a number of practical and psychological factors which may work against young people aged 11 to 17 being able to seek help when they experience maltreatment, even taking into account their typically increased competence to do so. These factors often meant that, at least initially, young people had sought help from family and peers rather than from professionals. This points to the important role played by informal supporters in helping young people access specialist professional help when needed.

Young people's accounts of their involvement in the child protection system also highlighted some of the challenges to professional practice with this age group of maltreated young people. First, issues of trust and confidentiality continued to be a key issue in young people's relationships with professionals. To illustrate this point, one young person recounted an incident where they had disclosed information to a professional, which was then shared with other family members:

> I thought that they were going to help me and not tell my mum when I told them stuff. … When my dad, yeah, he came to my new house, yeah. He hit my brother. I told [my social worker] not to say that I told … but then police came to my house and said, 'Your daughter said that this happened,' and my brother denied it … and it kicked off again. They [the police] went and it started again!
>
> (Young person aged 15, in Rees et al, 2010: 59)

A second related theme, evident in the above example, was the issue of young people's choice and control in the child protection process. This often went hand in hand with young people feeling their views were not listened to or adequately taken into account in professional decision-making.

Third, young people talked about feeling unclear about the roles of professionals in the child protection process and about what was happening at various points in time.

Finally, issues relating to accessibility of social work professionals and continuity of relationships were raised by young people. Perceived difficulties in accessing help at key moments and experience of having to work with a number of different social workers were both factors which presented barriers to the development of trusting relationships with professionals.

The implications of the government's response to the Munro Review for young people aged 11 to 17

In the first half of this chapter we have reviewed recent empirical research on the initial responses of child protection professionals in cases of suspected maltreatment of young people aged 11 to 17 in England. We now go on to consider the implications of the government's response to the Munro Review for future policy and practice in this area.

Much of the response to the Munro Review involves recommendations that are equally applicable to children and young people of all ages. However, there are a number of key themes in the government's response that have particular relevance for young people aged 11 to 17. We focus here on these themes as follows:

- a child-centred system;
- the renewed emphasis on professional judgement;
- developing social work expertise;
- localised responses;
- sharing responsibility for the provision of early help;
- evidence-based approaches and creating a learning system.

Overall, the Munro Review presents some significant opportunities for responding to some of the issues with the current child protection system in relation to older young people that we have identified through our research. However, there are also some risks, particularly bearing in mind that the implementation of developments following the review will take place in the context of significant cuts in overall expenditure on public services. While the child protection system itself may be protected from the impact of these cuts, the implications for other types of services for young people may erode some of the broader support network of services that are needed to provide a comprehensive safety net for young people at risk, incorporating primary, secondary and tertiary levels of intervention. With these issues in mind, we now turn to a discussion of the relevance of the key themes identified in relation to maltreated young people aged 11 to 17.

A child-centred system

A key overarching theme of the government's response to Munro relates to the concept of a child-centred system. One of the key characteristics envisaged in the government's response is a system with: 'children and young people's **wishes**, **feelings** and **experiences** placed at the centre' (DfE, 2011: 5, emphasis in original).

This is a very positive development, particularly given the experiences of the young people described above and the perceptions from professionals that one of the reasons the current system is not suitable for older young people relates to their lack of opportunities to participate. This seems a particularly important issue for this age group, given their typically increased competence and capacities. The government's response presents an opportunity to develop an improved system, which has young people's active participation as a fundamental principle.

In addition, in a child-centred system, consideration needs to be given to facilitating young people in seeking help and referring themselves to professional agencies. Young people at this age may be capable of doing this, particularly if they are given information. However, our research found that very few referrals were being received by children's social care through this route. The study referred to earlier on adolescent neglect, including research with young people (see Rees et al, 2011: 53–71), provides some pointers to potential approaches to tackle this issue. Messages from this research included the importance of tailoring information concisely for young people, focusing on key messages, providing information through a variety of means including multimedia and web-based materials, and the potential for providing universal information through schools.

Widespread provision of such information could also facilitate young people to assist friends who may be experiencing maltreatment.

A great deal also depends on young people's perceptions of the system and in particular some of the identified barriers to their seeking help – that is, trust and confidentiality. This raises a wider issue regarding information sharing, which may be a significant challenge to aspirations of a child-centred system. Our research indicates that there needs to be a careful balance between recognising the importance of trust and confidentiality in engaging and working effectively with older young people while also realising the need for appropriate information sharing between agencies when young people are facing high levels of risk.

The renewed emphasis on professional judgement

The Munro Review and the government's response identify the current system as having an 'over-standardised framework that makes it difficult for [frontline social workers] to prioritise time to form relationships with children and to understand their needs' (DfE, 2011: 7). Both documents envisage a situation where some layers of the current system are removed and social work professionals have greater scope to exercise judgement; they value professional expertise.

In the light of the above, our research has raised two issues that are relevant to consider. The first, discussed further below, is that this vision is dependent on the development of social work expertise to work with specific groups of children and young people. The second is that some of the barriers to working with older young people may be resource constraints and a perception that younger children should have priority for the resources that do exist. There is a risk that the emphasis on individual judgement will exacerbate this situation, particularly if practitioners are fearful of the consequences of exercising their judgement. As argued earlier, the child protection system and public discourse on child abuse and neglect are already highly sensitised to tragic cases involving younger children. This may serve to reduce further the focus on the needs of older young people if social work practitioners feel that the individual judgements they make will be held up to public scrutiny.

Developing social work expertise

The government's response to the review places emphasis on the development of professional expertise both within children's social care and within other professional groups. This is clearly an important priority for effectively responding to children's and young people's needs. Our research raises issues about current professional perceptions of the 'resilience' of older young people to maltreatment, which do not accord with research evidence on some of the specific negative outcomes of maltreatment for this age group cited earlier in this chapter. This suggests that it will be important that any new training and workforce development initiatives for existing social work staff, social work students and a broader range of professionals include consideration of the particular issues affecting young people of secondary school age who are experiencing maltreatment.

Localised responses

There is an emphasis in the Munro Review on localised responsibility for developing child protection responses:

> With the reduction of prescription, leaders in local authorities will have more autonomy but also more responsibility for helping their staff to operate with a high level of knowledge and skills. The review asks local authorities to take more responsibility for deciding the range of services they will offer, defining the knowledge and skills needed and helping the workers develop them. (Munro, 2011: 8)

This idea is in line with broader government thinking on localisation. On the basis of our research, this type of approach may carry both benefits and risks in relation to child protection work with older young people. There is evidence from our research that, prior to the Munro Review, local authorities were already developing diverse responses to the needs of this age group, based on their analysis of the difficulties with the current child protection system. These kinds of developments may lead to improved practice in relation to young people aged 11 to 17. On the other hand, our research also cited evidence of wide variations in child protection responses to this age group. There is a risk that, depending on local priorities, provision for maltreated young people will become subject to significant geographical inequalities. It will also be important that, as localised responses diverge, the learning from new initiatives and positive innovation is captured and shared to ensure that good practice becomes the norm.

Sharing responsibility for the provision of early help

The government response envisages the provision of 'effective help when a problem first arises at any stage in life' (DfE, 2011: 8). It is encouraging to see the specific acknowledgement in this response (and the quote cited earlier in this chapter) that early help is relevant across all age groups of children and young people. In this respect the Munro Review can provide an important stimulus for 'primary' interventions that seek to prevent or intervene early in situations where young people aged 11 to 17 may be at risk of maltreatment. It will be important that this discourse is continued in the future development of the child protection system and that there is no confusion between 'early intervention' and 'early years intervention'.

The government response sees a key role for a range of agencies in preventing child maltreatment:

> The Government wants to work with partners to create a radical change in the way local agencies coordinate their work to maximise existing resources and increase the range and number of preventative services on offer to children and families. (DfE, 2011: 8–9)

The comments made earlier in this section on the potential risks to the wider network of local services as a result of public spending cuts are particularly relevant here. Many primary interventions with this age group are provided by non-statutory services, and there is a risk that resource shortages will result in an erosion of these services, which may work against the stated aim of the government quoted above.

Finally, it is important to consider a wider range of interventions in relation to the maltreatment of older young people. While early interventions may often be successful, some young people will nevertheless have persistent issues within their home environments which require an ongoing response. It may be helpful therefore to see early intervention as one aspect of a continuum of response within, for example, a model of primary, secondary and tertiary intervention (see Rees et al, 2011: 89–104).

Evidence-based approaches and creating a learning system

Finally, there is a welcome emphasis in the Munro Review on evidence-based approaches to child protection practice and policy and the importance of creating a learning system. This is also pertinent to issues relating to the older age group of young people discussed in this chapter. Our literature review indicates that, internationally, there are currently substantial gaps in our understanding of child protection issues, and responses to them, in relation to young people aged 11 to 17. Therefore, in order for it to be possible to adopt an evidence-based approach to practice with this age group, there is an urgent need for further research to explore this issue. Priorities for research identified by our review of existing evidence are: first, an exploration of the specific background contextual risk and protective factors associated with the likelihood of maltreatment of this age group; and, second, evidence of evaluated interventions to meet the needs of this particular target group.

The government's response also envisages a key role for local safeguarding children boards (LSCBs) in monitoring and reviewing the quality and effectiveness of child protection interventions at a local level. Our research suggests that it is often difficult to access age-specific data on the workings of the child protection system. It will be important that LSCBs are able to access such information to ensure that there are appropriate processes and interventions in place for all age groups of children and young people.

Concluding comments

This chapter has summarised the current state of knowledge about child protection issues for young people aged 11 to 17, based on a review of international research and on two recent studies in England. This is a surprisingly under-researched topic and there are substantial gaps in the evidence, particularly in relation to the contexts associated with maltreatment of this age group and to a shortage of evaluated interventions. The international research evidence does, however, draw attention to the significant risk of negative outcomes associated with experiencing abuse or neglect in this age range – for example, those related to mental health, educational achievement and risk of involvement in offending.

In terms of responding to this issue, recent research in England has demonstrated that many professionals do not perceive the current child protection system and processes as best suited to meeting the needs of this particular age group. The Munro Review and the government's response provide an important opportunity to improve this situation. The chapter discusses the potential for this and also some of the risks. There are important issues to resolve in terms of professional knowledge of and expertise in the distinctive issues involved in maltreatment of older young people: the prioritisation of resources across different age groups of children, and generating and sharing learning about what works best in meeting the needs of young people aged 11 to 17 who experience maltreatment.

Notes

[1] Throughout this chapter we use the overarching term 'maltreatment' to refer to all forms of abuse and neglect.

[2] For example: Peter Connelly (aged 17 months) in 2007; Victoria Climbié (eight years old) in 2000; Leanne White (three years old) in 1992; Jasmine Beckford (four years old) in 1984; Maria Colwell (seven years old) in 1973.

[3] Both studies were undertaken jointly by researchers at the University of York, The Children's Society and the NSPCC.

[4] See www.nspcc.org.uk/neglectmatters

[5] The research component involving interviews with young people was conducted by Sarah Gorin and Alison Jobe at the NSPCC.

References

Brandon, M., Belderson, P., Warren, C., Howe, D., Gardner, R., Dodsworth, J. and Black, J. (2008) *Analysing child death and serious injury through abuse and neglect: What can we learn? A biennial analysis of serious case reviews, 2003–2005*, Research report RR023, Nottingham: DCSF.

Brandon, M., Bailey, S., Belderson, P., Gardner R., Sidebotham, P., Dodsworth, J., Warren, C. and Black, J. (2009) *Understanding serious case reviews and their impact: A biennial analysis of serious case reviews, 2005–2007*, Research report, RR129, London: Department for Children, Schools and Families (DCSF).

Collings, S.J. and Payne, M.F. (1991) 'Attribution of causal and moral responsibility to victims of father–daughter incest: an exploratory examination of five factors', *Child Abuse & Neglect*, 15, pp 513–21.

DfE (Department for Education) (2011) *A child-centred system: The government's response to the Munro Review of Child Protection*, London: The Stationery Office. Available at: www.education.gov.uk/publications.

Everson, M.D., Smith, J.B., Hussey, J.M., English, D., Litrownik, A.J., Dubowitz, H., Thompson, R., Knight, E.D. and Runyan, D.K. (2008) 'Concordance between adolescent reports of childhood abuse and child protection service determinations in an at-risk sample of young adolescents', *Child Maltreatment*, 31(1), pp 14–26.

Featherstone, B. and Evans, H. (2004) *Children experiencing maltreatment: Who do they turn to?* London: NSPCC.

Gorin, S. (2004) *Understanding what children say: Children's experiences of domestic violence, parental substance misuse and parental health problems*, London: National Children's Bureau (NCB).

Hicks, L. and Stein, M. (2010) *Neglect matters: A multi-agency guide for professionals working together on behalf of teenagers*, London: DCSF.

Maynard, C. and Wiederman, M. (1997) 'Undergraduate students' perceptions of child sexual abuse: effects of age, sex, and gender-role attitudes', *Child Abuse & Neglect*, 21(9), pp 833–44.

McGee, R.A., Wolfe, D.A., Yuen, S.A., Wilson, S.K. and Carnochan, J. (1995) 'The measurement of maltreatment: a comparison of approaches', *Child Abuse & Neglect*, 19(2), pp 233–49.

Munro, E. (2011) *The Munro Review of Child Protection: Final report: A child-centred system*, London: The Stationery Office. Available at: www.education.gov.uk/publications.

Rees, G., Wade, J., Franks, M. and Medforth, R. (2009) *Commissioning, delivery and perceptions of emergency accommodation for young runaways*, London: DCSF.

Rees, G., Gorin, S., Jobe, A., Stein, M., Medforth, R. and Goswami, H. (2010) *Safeguarding young people: Responding to young people aged 11–17 who are maltreated*, executive summary, London: The Children's Society.

Rees, G., Stein, M., Hicks, L. and Gorin, S. (2011) *Adolescent neglect: Research, policy and practice*, London: Jessica Kingsley.

Rogers, P. and Davies, M. (2007) 'Perceptions of victims and perpetrators in a depicted child sexual abuse case: gender and age factors', *Journal of Interpersonal Violence,* 22(5), pp 566–84.

Smith, C.A., Ireland, T.O. and Thornberry, T.P. (2005) 'Adolescent maltreatment and its impact on young adult antisocial behavior', *Child Abuse & Neglect*, 29(10), pp 1099–119.

Stein, M., Rees, G., Hicks, L. and Gorin, S. (2009) *Neglected adolescents – Literature review*, Research brief, London: DSCF.

Sternberg, K.J., Lamb, M.E., Guterman, E., Abbott, C.B. and Dawud-Noursi, S. (2005) 'Adolescents' perceptions of attachments to their mothers and fathers in families with histories of domestic violence: a longitudinal perspective', *Child Abuse & Neglect*, 29, pp 853–69.

Stewart, A., Livingston, M. and Dennison, S. (2008) 'Transitions and turning points: examining the links between child maltreatment and juvenile offending', *Child Abuse & Neglect*, 32, pp 51-66.

Thornberry, T.P., Ireland, T.O. and Smith, C.A. (2001) 'The importance of timing: the varying impact of childhood and adolescent maltreatment on multiple problem outcomes', *Development and Psychopathology*, 13(4), pp 957–79.

Thornberry, T.P., Henry, K.L., Ireland, T.O. and Smith, C.A. (2010) 'The causal impact of childhood-limited maltreatment and adolescent maltreatment on early adult adjustment', *Journal of Adolescent Health*, 46(4), pp 359–65.

Webster, S.W., O'Toole, R., O'Toole, A.W. and Lucal, B. (2005) 'Overreporting and underreporting of child abuse: teachers' use of professional discretion', *Child Abuse & Neglect*, 29, pp 1281–96.

Zellman, G.L. (1992) 'The impact of case characteristics on child abuse reporting decisions', *Child Abuse & Neglect*, 16, pp 57–74.

SEVEN

Serious case review

John Fox

> Whenever a child is deliberately injured or killed, there is inevitably great concern in case some important tell-tale sign has been missed. (Laming, 2003)

It is hard to argue against the simple idea that if a child has been deliberately killed or seriously harmed, society should do everything it can to learn whether safeguarding systems could be improved. The serious case review (SCR) process is fundamentally designed to do just that, yet it has become much maligned in recent years, with some commentators believing it is a weak process and others believing it is too heavily focused on apportioning blame. Since its introduction 20 years ago as the standard method of inquiry into the circumstances leading to cases in which children have died or been seriously harmed as a result of maltreatment, it has been possibly one of the most controversial aspects of the system used in England and Wales to safeguard children from abuse.

This chapter will explore whether a change of approach, as suggested by Professor Eileen Munro (Munro, 2011), might improve the outcomes in terms of learning and public confidence. It will also explore the relationship between the criminal justice system and the SCR and what happens when criminal proceedings are ongoing, and examine the role of independent people engaged in SCRs and how the voices of the child and family members are reflected in an SCR. It will, in effect, question whether changes to the current system are required.

A brief history

The government guidance *Working together under the Children Act 1989* (DH et al, 1991) first laid out the formal requirements for conducting SCRs. The document stressed the need for central government to be informed, so that public statements could be issued and developments reviewed, and offered seven principles to underpin the process: urgency, impartiality, thoroughness, openness, confidentiality, cooperation and resolution (Sinclair and Bullock, 2002).

For several years after their introduction it was not possible to establish exactly how many SCRs were commissioned on an annual basis, but Sinclair and Bullock (2002) estimated that there were likely to be around 90. Since 2007, when Ofsted took over the recording and scrutiny of SCRs, there has been a better central monitoring mechanism, and during the period between April 2007 and March 2009, 268 were conducted (Brandon et al, 2010), which equates to a likely current average of around 130 SCRs a year in England and Wales.

Although each SCR is used locally to improve safeguarding, the product of the review, known as the overview report, is also used to inform policymakers and improve practice nationally. Every two years an overview analysis of these reviews is commissioned by the government, the last published in 2010 (Brandon et al, 2010).

Why the controversy?

There are various reasons why some people are concerned about the current system of reviewing serious child abuse. While I do not necessarily share these concerns, it may be useful to set out some of the themes raised most frequently to understand why the system is now likely to be changed:

- **A blame culture?** The biennial review covering the period 2005 to 2007 attempted to establish how it felt for practitioners to be involved in a case that led to an SCR. The researchers commented that the SCR process adds to the 'lasting distress practitioners experience when involved with families where children die through abuse' (Brandon et al, 2009). The types of emotions highlighted by practitioner respondents to this research included guilt, worry about being made a scapegoat, fear and anxiety. Evidence submitted to Lord Laming for his progress report (2009) indicated: 'the primary purpose of SCRs as a learning process to protect children more effectively in the future is in danger of being lost. This is (partly) as a result both of confusion about the purpose of SCRs, which are sometimes perceived as holding individuals or agencies to account.'

- **Dominated by the Ofsted evaluation?** Before 2007, there was no national standard in terms of the evaluation of SCRs. Since April of that year, Ofsted has evaluated the SCR process in each case, as well as the individual components such as the overview report and the individual management review (IMR) reports. A grade is given on a four-point scale ranging from 'inadequate' to 'outstanding'. The standard required is very high and local safeguarding children boards (LSCBs) and directors of children's services must take remedial action if an SCR in their area is graded 'inadequate'. Indeed, in such cases, there may be a requirement for a complete or partial repetition of the SCR. One contributor to Lord Laming's progress report suggested: 'Ofsted are evaluating SCRs as if they were an academic exercise' (Laming, 2009). As a result of the evidence presented during his fact-finding exercise, Lord Laming wrote: 'Many of those who contributed to this report felt unsure about how Ofsted were making judgments on SCRs, or were concerned that too much emphasis was placed on the quality of the written report rather than on the SCR as an effective learning tool' (Laming, 2009).
- **Cost** Between 2003 and 2009, there was a large increase in the number of cases that were the subject of an SCR. Arguably, the substantial growth in the number of reviews diverts funds from operational services that can protect children (Brandon et al, 2010). The cold economic facts are that hard-pressed local authorities and LSCBs have to fund the reviews from their own budgets. To put this in perspective, it is quite possible that there could be a cost implication in the region of £30,000 to £50,000 for each SCR.

- **The learning is learnt** In chapter 6 of their most recent research study, Brandon et al (2010) examine the recurring themes emerging from that study and from their two previous studies conducted using the same methodology. There are many such themes. On the one hand this is quite depressing but on the other hand it begs the question *On a national level, are we learning anything new?* Indeed, the very first study conducted in the past decade by Sinclair and Bullock (2002) highlighted many of the themes still being identified as 'learning' points by the most recent biennial review. Of course, arguably, the primary stakeholders in any SCR are the local constituent agencies of the LSCB, so on that basis there may well be new learning in their area concerning training, practice or procedures, even if no new national learning is established.

Later in this chapter, I will explore ways in which the government has been invited to alter the way SCRs are conducted in order to address some of the themes outlined above. However, if any major changes are to be made, the legislation and guidance under which SCRs are conducted may also need to be changed.

The current law

Unlike a statutory inquiry, such as the Victoria Climbié Inquiry, individuals cannot be compelled to cooperate with or assist the SCR. Under the 2005 Inquiries Act, certain offences were created, such as the alteration or destruction of documents that may be required by an inquiry. This legislation does not apply to SCRs. However, under overarching legislation set out in the 2004 Children Act, some statutory agencies have a legal obligation to take part in the SCR, and perhaps by extension a duty to cooperate is also imposed upon employees of such organisations. A brief look at the law may help explain this.

LSCBs were established in accordance with a requirement in the 2004 Children Act. They are the key statutory mechanism for agreeing how the relevant organisations will cooperate to safeguard and promote the welfare of children, and for ensuring the effectiveness of what they do.

The role and function of LSCBs are set out in law by the 2006 Local Safeguarding Children Boards Regulations, statutory instrument 2006/90. Regulation 5 requires the LSCB to undertake an SCR when certain criteria are present. Procedures for carrying out SCRs are set out in chapter 8 of *Working together to safeguard children* (DfE, 2010), which prescribes:

> When a child dies (including death by suspected suicide) **and** abuse or neglect is known or suspected to be a factor in the death, the LSCB should **always** conduct a SCR into the involvement of organisations and professionals in the lives of the child and family.
>
> In addition, a SCR should always be carried out when a child dies in custody or any form of detention.
>
> In addition, LSCBs should consider whether to conduct a SCR whenever a child has been seriously harmed in the following situations:
>
> - a child sustains a potentially life-threatening injury or serious and permanent impairment of physical and/or mental health and development through abuse or neglect;
> - a child has been seriously harmed as a result of being subjected to sexual abuse;
> - a parent has been murdered and a domestic homicide review is being initiated under the Domestic Violence Crime and Victims Act 2004;
> - a child has been seriously harmed following a violent assault perpetrated by another child or an adult;
>
> **and** the case gives rise to concerns about the way in which local professionals and services worked together to safeguard and promote the welfare of children. This includes inter-agency and/or inter-disciplinary working.

Changes in the pipeline?

Having considered some of the perceived problems with the current system, it will be useful to examine an alternative approach.

When the Coalition government took power in May 2010, it commissioned Professor Eileen Munro to undertake a broad review of child protection and to make recommendations for improvements. In her findings, Munro (2011) recommended that there should be a systemic change to SCRs based on an approach used in sectors such as aviation and healthcare. The idea was that there should be less focus on what individuals did wrong and a greater focus on understanding the underlying issues that made professionals behave the way they did and what prevented them from being able to help and protect children properly; in other words, to move beyond identifying what happened to explain why it happened. This approach to reviews has been promoted by the Social Care Institute for Excellence (SCIE) and is known as 'systems methodology'.

What is not entirely clear is why Munro believes that the current system is not able to explain 'why' an event happened. She makes the point that 'hindsight bias has influenced the authors of many of the SCRs conducted when children, known to services, die or are seriously injured', although evidence for this claim is not established in the report. Arguably, under the current system, a good overview report author should be able to recognise the danger of 'hindsight bias', analyse the material made available, request more if necessary, establish the context in which people were working and answer the 'why' questions as well as the 'who'.

The government response to the Munro recommendations was published in July 2011 (DfE, 2011) and indicated that there may be a transition to the 'systems methodology' model and also an end to Ofsted evaluations. Although I believe that the spectre of the Ofsted evaluation has dominated the process too much, there has certainly been far more rigour and adherence to timescales since Ofsted started evaluating SCRs. It is important in my view that this is not lost.

It is sometimes overlooked that a suspicious child death is a type of 'domestic homicide'. In 2011, the requirement for domestic homicide reviews (DHRs) was established on a statutory basis under the 2004 Domestic Violence, Crime and Victims Act. To learn lessons when adults have been unlawfully killed during a domestic incident, the statutory guidance concerning DHRs (Home Office, 2011) prescribes a methodology which is identical in most respects to the guidance for SCRs contained in *Working together to safeguard children* (DfE, 2010), including the need for independent reviewers and IMRs by the agencies concerned.

The definition of domestic violence in the statutory guidance includes violence perpetrated against or involving partners, ex-partners, other relatives or household members. Certainly this would seem to mean that children killed in the household by a carer would fall within this definition, yet there is no requirement to carry out a DHR if the victim is less than 17 years old. Presumably this is because the government is satisfied that the current arrangements for conducting SCRs under *Working together* (DfE, 2010) are robust and fit for purpose. It would seem incongruous, however, for reviews on the deaths of *children* within a household to be less robust and far-reaching than reviews on older siblings or relatives. Perhaps, if the arrangements for conducting SCRs are to be changed, the 'systems model' should only apply to cases that don't involve the *death* of a child and the current SCR model retained for when the death of a child has occurred due to maltreatment?

Aside from that philosophical point, there are some practical considerations concerning a change to the 'systems model':

- Older cases or those with a longitudinal timespan might be very difficult to review because the professionals involved would no longer be around, or would have forgotten the case and the context at the time.
- Training for local review teams is part of the requirement and could be expensive (for example, to learn the required qualitative research skills to degree level would normally take a year).
- The proposed group of nationally accredited independent reviewers may not have the skill base to understand the subtle aspects of agency responses, bearing in mind they will not be informed by an IMR report and robust analysis by an expert in their particular field.

- Arrangements for involving families and significant others might be made more difficult.
- Engaging the professionals involved in a case to ascertain the context in which they worked is very important. But in a large meeting of senior and junior staff from all agencies, a distorted picture could emerge: people may feel unhappy or unable to speak in an open forum, or they might not wish publicly to blame colleagues or other agencies. The current system of a private meeting with the IMR reviewer might be less threatening to some key staff.
- If a large uncontrolled meeting of relevant practitioners were convened as part of a 'systems model' review, a parallel criminal investigation (see below) might be more likely to be compromised. Material generated on 'post-its', rough notes, flip charts, and so on, would be harder to assess for relevance and the requirement for disclosure.
- It is unlikely that lawyers and insurers would agree to staff being allowed to speak openly on such an 'awayday', especially if the review were dealing with a controversial or high-profile case (for example, Peter Connelly).
- Individual agencies would lose the opportunity to conduct a robust internal review under the current controlled system (IMR).

Public confidence

Public interest in safeguarding children is evident from a number of recent SCRs. In the context of tragedies involving children, the way the public feels does matter, not least because public services are accountable to the communities they serve. The apparent importance that the public and the media attach to a robust examination when a tragedy involving a child occurs may be an inconvenience but it cannot be ignored. The public, and the media, demand a robust SCR process in which they have confidence.

A briefing paper produced by a researcher at the University of Edinburgh revealed:

> The overwhelming interest in details surrounding the death of Peter Connelly (Baby P) is exemplified by the number of UK newspaper articles which mentioned the case. A search of the Lexus Library Database found that there were 2832 mentions of the Baby P case in UK newspapers from 1st November 2008 to 1st November 2009. The tabloid newspaper *The Sun* alone printed 848 articles mentioning the case during that year. (Elsey, 2010, p 1)

The briefing paper went on to describe how 'most of the print media in this first phase of reporting' commented that this 'was evidence of professional and system failure' and 'the line of reporting, particularly in the tabloid press, was that the professional had not carried out their duties effectively' (Elsey, 2010, p 5). In its editorials in the wake of the death of Peter Connelly, *The Sun* regularly demanded the sacking of the director of children's services in the London borough concerned.

Presumably to increase public confidence in the system, from June 2010, the government decided to publish full SCR overview reports rather than just the executive summary. It is too early to know what the full impact of this might be but it could mean that some lessons are not learnt. As set out earlier in this chapter, unlike a full statutory inquiry, an SCR cannot require practitioners to cooperate with the review, so the laudable aspiration to make the review process more transparent and robust may make practitioners more fearful of being open and honest about their role in the events surrounding the incident in question. Even though attempts are made to anonymise individuals, the reality is that for an overview report to be of any use it has to contain detail, the inclusion of which can easily lead to revealing the identity of key individuals, whether they are named or not.

Whatever the merits or otherwise of publishing the full overview report, the genie is now out of the bottle. If an attempt is made to reverse this decision, the media are likely, in high-profile cases, to be dissatisfied with the apparent lack of specific answers as to why an individual case went wrong.

The role of independent people

Although some LSCBs have traditionally commissioned independent people to lead the SCR process, the idea was formalised by Lord Laming in *The protection of children in England* (2009). It is now a requirement that each SCR will be led by two independent safeguarding experts, one to act as the chair of the SCR panel and one to analyse the evidence and write an overview report. Laming seemed content that there could be a single independent person because he wrote: 'an SCR author may or may not be the same person who chairs the SCR panel' (Laming, 2009). However, subsequent guidance in *Working together* (DfE, 2010) requires that the chair of any SCR panel should not also be the overview report author, thereby creating the requirement for two independent people to be commissioned for the SCR. Neither of these independent people is 'in charge' of the process as such, but each has a distinct role to play.

The panel chair

The SCR panel chair manages the 'business' side of the SCR. This includes leading on the membership and structure of the SCR panel and drafting the terms of reference. They set the agenda, chair all panel meetings and are responsible for robust timekeeping at meetings. They should liaise closely with the LSCB business manager and monitor communications between the SCR and the LSCB chair and other agency leads. Where a criminal investigation is under way, they should meet with the police senior investigator and, if appropriate, the Crown Prosecutor to discuss how each process can be carried out without hindrance to the other. They should ensure that sufficient time is allowed in the overall six months' timespan for the overview report author to carry out a robust analysis of the agency IMR reports and produce a first draft report. The chair should then ensure that all panel members have the opportunity to comment on and suggest alterations to the overview report.

The overview report author

The independent author should be appointed early enough to contribute to the terms of reference and the decision on which agencies will be asked to provide an IMR. The author should have an early meeting with the IMR reviewers and be satisfied that they are of sufficient seniority to challenge their organisation, were not operationally involved the case and do not line-manage any practitioners who were. On receipt of the IMR reports, they should conduct a robust analysis of the case, highlight any areas of inconsistency in the IMR reports from different agencies and seek to reconcile these. They should take responsibility for meeting family members and significant others to increase learning opportunities. They should produce a first draft of the overview report and LSCB recommendations for the panel to consider as soon as possible, and be prepared to listen to the views of the panel in respect of factual inaccuracies. They should present the report and recommendations to the full LSCB and attend any event organised by the LSCB to assist with the dissemination of learning.

Why should families be involved in SCRs?

For an SCR to be effective, the process must uncover all the material and evidence which could lead to greater learning about how services for children and families could be improved. Professionals will have their views and their contribution is of course vital, but professionals may not always understand how the end user feels about the service they were offered or given.

In their 2005–07 biennial analysis (Brandon et al, 2009), plenty of evidence was cited indicating the value and necessity of involving families and the community in the learning process. And in every SCR I have been commissioned to undertake, my analysis of agency involvement and the service provided has been greatly assisted by the involvement of family members and significant others. Arguably, the most important learning can come from family, friends, neighbours and so on. The concept of 'involving families' should never be considered a tick-box exercise; it should be a central part of every SCR.

Apart from learning how the family viewed the services they were offered, it is also sometimes crucial for the review to understand the hostility that professionals may have faced while trying to safeguard a child. In one case, through personally meeting the carer of a child who had been seriously sexually abused, I was able to understand that the social workers and others trying to operate within that family environment were up against a manipulative and devious parent who would undoubtedly have made every attempt to thwart plans and cover up the abuse happening to the child. This particular parent, who has since been convicted in the criminal court, lied consistently during our discussion and attempted to blame others, including professionals, for the abuse to her child. When writing my subsequent overview report and conducting the analysis, I was able to draw on my own experience of trying to 'work with' this particular parent. This gave me the opportunity to empathise with the frontline professionals while questioning why their supervisors did not do more to understand how impossible it was for social workers and health visitors to work in a meaningful way with that family.

During the Victoria Climbié Inquiry, Victoria's murderer, her aunt, performed in a similar way while giving her evidence to Lord Laming. She was bombastic and hostile and blamed the doctors at a hospital for killing Victoria, despite the overwhelming evidence of long-term, systematic torture. This spectacle gave the inquiry team a greater understanding of what it must have been like for the many frontline professionals attempting to work with this woman.

It is sometimes stressful to meet with someone whom one can predict will be hostile and manipulative, and it may be tempting to try to avoid it. However, it does a disservice to those professionals potentially subject to criticism if the context of the family with whom they were trying to work is not fully understood by those carrying out the review.

I also believe that, in many cases, families benefit in an emotional and perhaps therapeutic sense from being involved in the SCR process. Where I have spoken to family members, they have generally expressed the view that they were glad to have been asked to take part and I believe their experience was positive. It would be understandable if some family members had a default position of expecting the SCR to be a non-transparent process, perhaps overly weighted towards protecting the 'authorities' from blame. I have found that by meeting even apparently hostile family members, I have been able to reassure them and give them confidence in the independent and transparent nature of the SCR.

The involvement not only of the family but also of 'significant others' is a particularly important concept. For example, in a particular case, a neighbour had repeatedly contacted children's services and the police to report suspected child abuse perpetrated against a child who was subsequently killed, but she was treated like a nuisance caller because she was reluctant to give her name. Speaking to this woman could have revealed a lot about what it feels like for a concerned neighbour, in this case living in a run-down and intimidating social housing estate, to pluck up the courage to alert the statutory agencies, only to be repeatedly ignored.

In respect of families, we need to know how they felt when dealing with the relevant agencies and whether they fully understood what they were being asked to do. For example, in another case, a mother with mild learning difficulties was asked to sign a voluntary contract to prevent a paedophile boyfriend coming into her home; she was being portrayed as being culpable in her daughter's sexual abuse. But a conversation with her revealed that she was hopelessly unable to meet the terms of the written agreement and it was written in such professional jargon that she didn't understand the terms anyway.

The only hindrance that cannot be overcome is when a family member refuses to get involved. If they are prepared to help the SCR learn lessons, nothing should prevent it. It is just a matter of timing, and the perception that SCR reviewers cannot interview witnesses or even defendants in a criminal case is simply wrong. There should be an assumption that the SCR will interview anyone who can help maximise learning. However, discussion must take place with the police and CPSabout when this should take place. For example, if a parent is on bail pre-charge and the police are planning to re-interview them after forensic results come back, I believe that it is best for the SCR-based conversation to take place after the police have finished interviewing.

In their earlier biennial analysis (Brandon et al, 2009), the researchers reveal that fairly flimsy reasons are sometimes given for failing to involve families. In one report examined, they discovered the comment: 'Due to police proceedings – unable to contact parents to ask if they wish to be involved.' On the face of it, this seems an unacceptable approach, which should have been challenged by the SCR panel. Families, and where possible children, should *always* be invited to get involved in the SCR; the only discussion should be about timing.

Children themselves can give valuable information, but a direct conversation with the independent author could be problematic as it may reopen traumatic memories. Professionals are often carrying out direct work with such children and one imaginative approach to gain some learning from children might be to ask their caseworkers to include relevant questions in their regular sessions.

Post-review, I believe that it is the responsibility of the panel chair and perhaps the LSCB chair to meet key family members to explain what learning has been gained from the review, although occasionally I have taken on this responsibility in my role as overview report author.

Criminal proceedings running alongside SCRs

Working together (DfE, 2010) acknowledges that when an SCR is commissioned and there is a current ongoing police investigation or pending prosecution involving some of the relevant parties, there may be a need for compromise either in terms of the timescales during which the SCR is completed or concerning the activity carried out by the people conducting the SCR.

It may be useful to consider the following principles, which underpin any discussions between the 'prosecution team' (the police and the CPS) and the SCR panel chair:

- Both SCRs and criminal investigations are important processes to safeguard children and neither should be compromised if at all possible.
- It is important that criminal prosecutions are carried out in a 'just' manner and therefore nothing done by the SCR should cause or allow a miscarriage of justice.
- For the SCR to be effective, *all* possible learning needs to be established in order to safeguard children immediately and in the future, and the existence of a criminal investigation should not compromise that learning.

From the point of view of the police and CPS, the main concern is likely to be that the SCR team might need to interview potential prosecution witnesses or defendants, and in so doing their evidence could be compromised. Criminal cases can take many months or even years to be finalised, and because those conducting the SCR are working towards a six-month deadline, there can sometimes be a conflict of interests which the two sides need to work through.

There is a real need for dialogue between the senior police officer conducting the criminal enquiry and the SCR panel chair because it is unlikely that both will fully understand the working procedures and requirements of each respective process.

In April 2011, a guidance document (ACPO/CPS, 2011) was published by the police, the CPS and two LSCBs to help parties deal with any conflict and create an environment whereby both processes could not only successfully run alongside each other but might even assist each other. This is recommended further reading.

One of the concerns for the prosecution team is likely to be that material generated by the SCR, such as interview notes by IMR reviewers, could contain new evidence or comments that might taint the reputation of prosecution witnesses. If, for example, a potential defendant were interviewed for an SCR, they might say something that contradicted a police interview. Likewise, a potential prosecution witness might give a different version of events than they gave in a police statement, or information may be uncovered by the SCR that might lead to doubt about their truthfulness, which of course would be highly relevant if a jury had to rely on their evidence in court.

The 1996 Criminal Procedure and Investigations Act (CPIA), including its code of practice, and the Attorney General's guidelines on the disclosure of information in criminal proceedings govern the disclosure of unused material to the defence. This means material that may be relevant to the investigation and has been retained but does not form part of the case against the accused. It is advantageous for any SCR panel chair to understand the CPIA and its implications.

The code requires the police to record and retain all material obtained *during their investigation* which may be relevant to the case. The CPIA defines what is meant by a 'criminal investigation' and an SCR does not fall within the scope of that definition. However, any material generated by an SCR is classed as 'third-party material' and the police must carry out reasonable enquiries to establish whether such material exists and, if so, whether it might be relevant to the criminal prosecution.

The CPS should initially treat all SCR documents as 'sensitive material', and as such this should not appear on any schedule provided to the defence. This is a key safeguard and means that, although the police may have been allowed to view SCR material which they believe is relevant, the SCR panel chair will still be 'in control' of its dissemination. It should not be disclosed to the defence unless the SCR panel chair agrees or has had the chance to instruct solicitors to argue in court that it would not be in the public interest for it to be disclosed.

The fact that someone has made a witness statement to the police, or even that someone has been interviewed as a suspect or is charged with an offence, would not in itself preclude the SCR review team from seeking to obtain from them any learning which could help protect children at that time or in the future. This may involve a personal interview or a request for a contribution to the SCR in writing. However, if interviews are conducted with people who may be involved in criminal proceedings, the police and CPS should be informed so that they can discharge their disclosure duties under the CPIA. Seeking to delay or restrict the work of an SCR, and therefore the learning it achieves, may sometimes be necessary, but it should be seen as a grave step which may prejudice the welfare of children.

Conclusion

My stance remains that the current SCR process stands up to the test when evaluated against the alleged shortcomings outlined at the start of this chapter. SCRs are independent, rigorous inquiries that are able to provide learning for both local practice and national policy. I believe that the evaluation provided by Ofsted, albeit at times unwieldy, has brought an additional layer of independence and scrutiny to the process. To throw the baby out with the bathwater may undermine public confidence that LSCBs and local statutory agencies have worked so hard to win since the outcry over the Peter Connelly case in 2009. If a child dies within a family because of maltreatment, any review has to be *at least* as rigorous as the DHR, which must now, by law, be conducted if an older family member dies.

It is early days for the 'systems model' and it is not clear how the implementation of the new methodology will be resourced or initiated. SCRs are already expensive and resource-intensive, and any change in the system should not add to the burden already carried by hard-pressed local authorities and statutory agencies.

It is perfectly possible to conduct an SCR alongside criminal proceedings and still seek learning from family members, even if they are witnesses or defendants. It is simply a matter of timing. To achieve harmony, those involved in the SCR and in the police investigation must communicate and understand and respect what each process needs to achieve.

References

ACPO/CPS (Association of Chief Police Officers/Crown Prosecution Service) (2011) *A guide for the police, the CPS and local safeguarding children boards to assist with liaison and the exchange of information when there are simultaneous Chapter 8 SCRs and criminal proceedings*, London: ACPO.

Brandon, M., Bailey, S., Belderson, P., Gardner, R., Sidebotham, P., Dodsworth, J., Warren, C. and Black, J. (2009) *Understanding serious case reviews and their impact: A biennial analysis of serious case reviews 2005–2007*, London: The Stationery Office.

Brandon, M., Bailey, S. and Belderson, P. (2010) *Building on the learning from serious case reviews: A two-year analysis of child protection database notifications 2007–2009*, London: The Stationery Office.

DfE (Department for Education) (2010) *Working together to safeguard children*, London: The Stationery Office.

DfE (2011) *A child-centred system: The government's response to the Munro Review of Child Protection*, London: The Stationery Office. Available at: www.education.gov.uk/publications.

DH (Department of Health), Department of Education and Science and the Welsh Office (1991) *Working together under the Children Act 1989*, London: HMSO.

Elsey, S. (2010) *Media coverage of child deaths in the UK: The impact of Baby P: A case for influence?*, Edinburgh: Centre for Learning in Child Protection.

Home Office (2011) *Multi-agency statutory guidance for the conduct of domestic homicide reviews*, London: The Stationery Office.

Laming, Lord (2003) *The Victoria Climbié Inquiry report*, London: The Stationery Office.

Laming, Lord (2009) *The protection of children in England: A progress report*, London: The Stationery Office.

Munro, E (2011) *The Munro Review of Child Protection: Final report*, London: The Stationery Office. Available at: www.education.gov.uk/publications.

Sinclair, R. and Bullock, R. (2002) *Learning from past experience: A review of serious case reviews*, London: DH.

Conclusion

Enver Solomon and Maggie Blyth

Since the tragic death of Victoria Climbié in 2000, the child protection system has been subject to constant public and political scrutiny. Laming's damning indictment that there was 'widespread organisational malaise' (Laming, 2003) led to new legislation and a fundamental overhaul, with the creation of children's services, local safeguarding children boards (LSCBs) and procedural reform, including the publication of interagency guidance *Working together to safeguard children* (DfE, 2010). These changes had barely begun to be implemented when further proposals were made by another inquiry following the death of Baby Peter in 2007. The emphasis was more on workforce reform in order 'to translate policy, legislation and guidance into day-to-day practice on the frontline of every service' (Laming, 2009). It was expected that these reforms would be given some opportunity to bed down. But this wasn't to be.

In May 2010, the Coalition government appointed a children's minister, Tim Loughton, with a keen interest in the child protection system. In opposition, he had set up a Commission on the Future of British Social Workers which reported to the second Laming Inquiry that 'no amount of reforms and procedures will succeed unless they free up properly trained, motivated and resourced social workers and other key professionals to get on with their job of working with families at the "sharp end", based on maximising quality face to face time with the vulnerable families' (Conservative Party, 2009). In government, Loughton has instigated a significant policy shift on the basis that ongoing reforms borne out of tragedy have not helped frontline child protection workers do their job better. Instead, they have hindered them:

> Over the years, individual child tragedies have prompted national reviews and inquiries, resulting in calls for action. In response, legislation has been passed; rulebooks have expanded; more procedures and processes have been

> introduced and structures have been changed. But the fundamental problems have not gone away. Despite the very best of intentions, hard-working social workers, foster carers and other frontline professionals are, too often, still not able to make the difference they want to for vulnerable children and families. Day in day out they are up against a system that simply does not help them to do their best for children. (DfE, 2011a: 2)

Not surprisingly, shortly after taking office, Loughton asked Professor Eileen Munro to undertake a further independent review of the child protection system. Current government policy is determined to provide a child protection system with 'less central prescription and interference, where we place greater trust and responsibility in skilled professionals at the front line' (DfE, 2011a). As set out in the contributions in this volume, delivering this reform through the Munro recommendations brings a number of overlapping challenges. These include: the capacity of the workforce; diminishing public sector resources; the future of early intervention approaches and partnership working; the risk of unintended consequences; and the impact of wider reforms affecting health and schools.

Can the workforce deliver?

The delivery of the Munro reforms very much depends on two principles – the capacity and ability of frontline practitioners to deliver, and how local authorities reconfigure specialist services, including those responsible for child protection and vulnerable children, young people and families. Current social worker vacancy rates indicate that, in children services, 8% of posts remain unfilled (*Community Care*, 2011). Although the vacancy rate is declining, reports suggest that some local authorities have restructured, thereby reducing the number of posts rather than employing more staff (*Community Care*, 2011).

The Munro Review will certainly require new ways of working in child protection services for all multi-agency staff at the 'front door', with social workers expected to place more emphasis on professional judgement and health practitioners expected to play a greater part in child protection. An expanded health visitor workforce, for example, working closely with children's centres, is anticipated to be part of the improved early warning system for social workers. Given the planned recruitment targets for health visitors (4,200 nationally), this could be particularly challenging. Moreover, if social workers are subject to less guidance and have greater discretion, will this result in more effective child protection planning across the partnership? Whether or not staff can change practice after many years of having to adopt a more prescriptive approach is open to question. If health visitors are to have a greater part in the child protection system, sufficient numbers need to be recruited and they need to be adequately trained. The success of the Munro reforms hinges on frontline staff being given continuous professional support so that they are skilled in reviewing risk. It also requires the entire multi-agency partnership to have a common understanding of thresholds and agreed multi-agency protocols on levels of need in local areas. How will frontline practitioners, whether social workers, health visitors, midwives, teachers or police officers, ensure that all children get the right response at the right time?

As Jenny Clifton notes in Chapter 3, 'without a good grasp of each child's worries and of the impact of the family dynamics on them, professionals will not have the child's voice as a central focus'. To truly bring the voice of the child to the forefront of practice, as Munro would like, will clearly require a very different way of working. In particular, there will need to be a new approach to multi-agency training that places emphasis on the child's journey and ensures that an offer of 'early help' is available for all children in need. Furthermore, if the inspection framework, as Munro proposes and Ofsted accepts, is to examine the effectiveness of all agencies involved in the child's case and to incorporate the journey of the child, including their views and wishes, there will need to be a radically different way of working. Locality teams, multi-agency frontline partnerships and the 'MASH'[1] approaches, as Munro highlights, will be required to ensure swift exchange of information, assessment and intervention from prevention services through to child protection conferences. It is important too that this is applied to older vulnerable young people as well as children affected by parental mental health, substance misuse or violence (Coombe, Chapter 4; Holt, Chapter 5; Stein and Rees, Chapter 6).

Resourcing at a time of rising demand

In any analysis of the government's response to Munro it is hard not to conclude that the question of resourcing at a time of rising demand has become the elephant in the room. Latest figures show that the number of children in care is the highest it has been since 1987 and the number of children on child protection orders has risen by 14,000 in the past five years (DfE, 2011b; 2011c). Yet children's social care budgets are much reduced. The early intervention grant, which incorporates all non-ring-fenced money for children's services, has been cut by 24% in real terms when compared to the equivalent spend before the Coalition government came to power. Overall, local authorities have seen their budgets substantially reduced for each of the four years between 2011 and 2014. So there is less money available and the demand for resources is rising. And there is every reason to believe that it will continue to rise. The economic recession shows no sign of coming to an end very soon and cuts to welfare support will hit those on lowest incomes with children. For example, the proposed cap on benefits will affect over 200,000 children, potentially forcing many of them into poverty. The number of vulnerable children is already on the rise, with 200,000 more children living in poverty compared to 2004 (Institute for Fiscal Studies, 2011).

The Munro Review fails to address how to benchmark thesholds. In Chapter 1, Colin Green notes that the reality of financial pressures makes the job of delivering early help 'very unpromising'. The government wants universal services to be reconfigured so that they identify vulnerable children and their families more effectively. Many areas have responded with an emphasis on shared services between health and social care and multi-agency safeguarding teams. However, services vary across local authority areas, and with significant changes still occurring in the health economy and education, the ability of universal services to play a greater role in identifying and meeting need before crisis point is arguably curtailed.

Laming remarked in his inquiry into Victoria Climbié's death that lack of funds and inadequate staffing were a factor (Laming, 2003). If the ultimate aim of Munro is to improve outcomes for children, there must be acknowledgement from government that children's social services cannot achieve this without investment in early intervention and support from partners, including the third sector. Greater honesty is required, so that there are realistic expectations about what can and cannot be delivered. The ability of agencies to deliver early help must also be reappraised.

Munro – the unintended consequences

All reforms carry the risk of unintended consequences. As contributors writing for this volume show, there are some profound risks attached to the Munro proposals that remain unaddressed in the government response. This leaves uncertainty about how successfully Munro's recommendations will be incorporated into child protection policy and practice.

Criticism of drift in child protection decision-making and lack of throughput in reviewing child protection planning is a constant theme arising from Ofsted inspections (Ofsted, 2011). Indeed, at present, children's social care is being criticised for not taking timely decisions in adoption cases (Narey, 2011), and Ofsted data published during 2011 (Ofsted, 2011) show that nearly one quarter of local authority safeguarding services have been deemed 'inadequate'. It is perhaps surprising therefore that Munro and the government are happy to see targets for decision-making removed. They want good quality decision-making to be the primary driver and believe that timeliness targets undermine this goal. But there is a real danger that the pendulum could swing back, preventing improvement and leading to drift in case management. Rather than dismiss the gains that have been made in achieving more timely decisions, there needs to be an emphasis on achieving a balance between quality and timeliness.

As well as the danger of delay creeping back into the system, there is also the possibility that there could be a far greater variation in practice. Munro actively promotes less central control and greater professional autonomy. She also wants far less central prescription in assessment and decision-making. Local areas are encouraged to adopt the processes they see as most effective. The inevitable risk is that there will be much more variation in practice. One of the reasons behind the creation of the common assessment framework (CAF) was to avoid this so that there was a standard expectation of what should happen regardless of local pressures. This will now change, and there is evidence in the structural reform already under way, with a third of areas opting not to have a dedicated director of children's services (Association of Directors of Children's Services, 2011), that local areas will quickly adopt their own approaches.

From safeguarding to child protection?

The final report of the Munro Review does not include the word 'safeguard' or 'safeguarding' once. Given that it is called the Munro Review of *Child Protection* (emphasis added), this is not necessarily surprising. However, it is significant in that it could mark a shift from the notion that children need to be safeguarded by all agencies. Instead, there is a danger that child protection will be framed as primarily being the business of children's social care.

The Every Child Matters reforms were intended to embed child protection into the work of all professionals who have a role in keeping children safe. At the heart was partnership working, particularly with police, education and health. There has been progress in achieving this, although, as Michael Preston-Shoot highlights in his review of LSCBs in Chapter 2, it is rather patchy and far from perfect. Yet Munro is very weak in stating the need to join up her proposed reforms with the changes under way in health and education. Coombe (Chapter 4) emphasises the risk of fragmentation resulting from the NHS reforms. Inevitably, child protection or safeguarding may no longer be regarded as everybody's business but will be left to children's social care.

First, school reforms focus primarily on educational attainment. There is little reference to the importance of schools contributing to a child's overall health and wellbeing. It was only when the Lords intervened, with the support of influential lobby groups, that the proposed removal of the duty on schools to cooperate with local authorities in relation to safeguarding was overturned in October 2011. Despite this amendment, the framework for schools remains very narrow, concentrating on raising standards and curriculum reform rather than addressing schools' responsibilities in meeting the welfare needs of their pupils.

Second, the health reforms are in danger of entirely overlooking the needs of children. As currently configured, the health reforms will disrupt the established safeguarding mechanisms for children, but it is not clear how safeguarding will be integrated into all commissioning decisions for children in future, particularly in relation to designated professionals in the health service. Coombe touches on this in Chapter 4. What is more, despite Munro's welcomed emphasis on the voice of the child, it has not been given the same prominence in the health reforms.

Third, it is not clear how the police reforms and the creation of police and crime commissioners will influence the organisation of public protection units and whether there will be reduced availability for partnership working in the area of child protection. Fox in Chapter 7 points out that there has been good progress in integrating SCR outcomes with criminal investigations in the past couple of years. It is important that this is not forgotten in a revised focus on learning lessons where children are harmed or die.

Overall, there is little in Munro or the government's response that addresses the importance of joining up the reform agendas to deliver effective partnership working. This appears to be reflective of a move away from the broader safeguarding agenda to a more narrow focus on child protection. But will this deliver better outcomes for children? Joined-up working was given priority specifically because it was felt that agencies had failed to work together, contributing to high-profile failures. Moving away from this agenda will surely risk putting the clock back to when interagency working was failing to protect children adequately.

Where next for child protection?

Many professionals have hailed the Munro Review as a welcome new beginning in which trust and faith are restored in their professional judgement. However, when drilling down into the detail, do the reforms go far enough in what they demand of national policy and local practice? As the contributions in this volume highlight, the issues stir considerable debate and the thrust of Munro's recommendations are in danger of losing momentum due to other upheavals in the public sector and a lack of evidence base. Enhancing professional judgement, reducing bureaucracy and placing responsibility for improvement at the local level may sound enticing. Yet conversely, without resources, there are real questions about the sustainability of LSCBs as effective partnership bodies able to provide scrutiny of the 'front door'. The outlook for the early help offer is sound, but the evidence will need to be gathered and the data examined to ensure that services are truly effective in engaging children, young people and their families, Finally, and most important, the judgement for the Munro Review will lie in its contribution to the outcomes and experience of those children and young people caught up in the child protection system.

Note

[1] The MASH (Multi-Agency Safeguarding Hub) was set up in Devon in June 2010 as a forum bringing all agencies together including police, probation, fire, ambulance, health, education and social care through co-location and sharing information to determine the most appropriate intervention to respond to a child's need and to trigger an immediate response to the child and their family to prevent harm. It is now being piloted in different parts of the country.

References

Association of Directors of Children's Services (2011) *New futures: What is happening to children's services?*, Manchester: ADCS.

Community Care (2011) 'Vacancy rates down across Britain as councils strive to protect posts', 22 September.

Conservative Party (2009) *Conservative Party Commission on Social Workers: Response to Lord Laming's Inquiry*, London: Conservative Party.

DfE (Department for Education) (2010) *Working together to safeguard children: A guide to inter-agency working to safeguard and promote the welfare of children*, London: The Stationery Office.

DfE (2011a) *A child-centred system: The government's response to the Munro Review of Child Protection*, London: The Stationery Office. Available at: www.education.gov.uk/publications.

DfE (2011b) *Children looked after in England (including adoption and care leavers), year ending 31 March 2011*, London: DfE.

DfE (2011c) *Referrals, assessments and children who were the subject of a child protection plan (2010/11 Children in Need census, provisional)*, London: DfE.

Institute for Fiscal Studies (2011) *Child and working age poverty and inequality in UK: 2010*, London: Institute of Fiscal Studies.

Laming (2003) *The Victoria Climbié Inquiry*, London: HMSO.

Laming (2009) *The protection of children in England: A progress report*, London: HMSO.

Narey (2011) *The Narey Report: A blueprint for the nation's lost children*, London: The Times.

Ofsted (2011) *Annual Report of Her Majesty's Chief Inspector of Education, Children's Services and Skills 2009//10*, London: Ofsted.

Index

Page references for notes are followed by n

D

E

F

G

H

I

J

K

L

M